J15

JUNIOR NATURE GUIDE
SEA LIFE

Written by Leslie Jackman

www.alligatorbooks.co.uk

Collector's Code

Remember that beaches can be dangerous places as well as pleasant ones.

1 Always go collecting with a friend, and always tell an adult where you are going.

2 Keep a careful eye on the tide and make sure you can reach safety if it starts to come in.

3 Avoid damaging the environment or harming any living creature you come across.

4 Keep to footpaths as much as possible.

5 Ask permission before crossing private property to reach a beach or going on a private landing stage.

6 Take your litter home.

© 2007 Alligator Books Limited
Published by Alligator Books Limited
Gadd House, Arcadia Avenue,
London N3 2JU

Printed in Malaysia

Contents

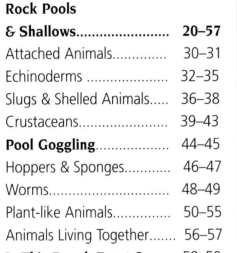

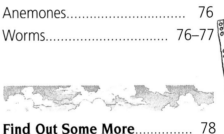
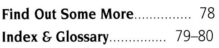

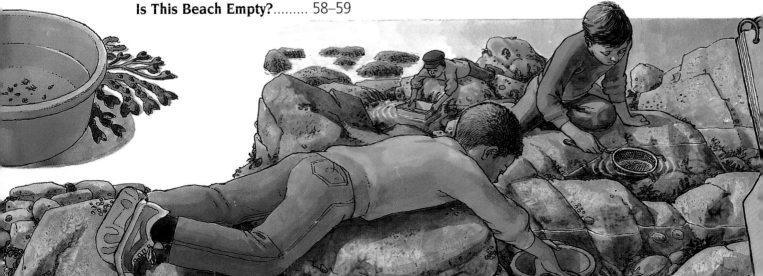

What Is Out There?

An amazing variety of animals live in the sea from tiny shrimps to the largest animal on Earth – the Great Blue Whale. Life started in the sea and spread from there to fresh water, and finally on to the land about 400 million years ago.

You can find marine animals on almost any sort of seashore, but rocky shores have the greatest variety. This book will show you the animals that you are most likely to find because they live on the seashore, or may be seen when you are out in a boat.

Animals living on the seashore have a hard time. When the tide goes out, they may be exposed for many hours to hot sunshine or freezing cold. Most marine animals have gills and can only breathe in water. So some species close up tightly and keep some water inside their shells. Others hide in rock pools or under boulders where water remains.

Barnacle lifecycle

Many marine animals reproduce by shedding their eggs into the water. The eggs eventually hatch out into larvae which often look nothing like the adult. These minute larvae are part of the plankton and many get eaten. Those that survive may drift for many miles, but eventually they settle down on the sea bed and change into adults.

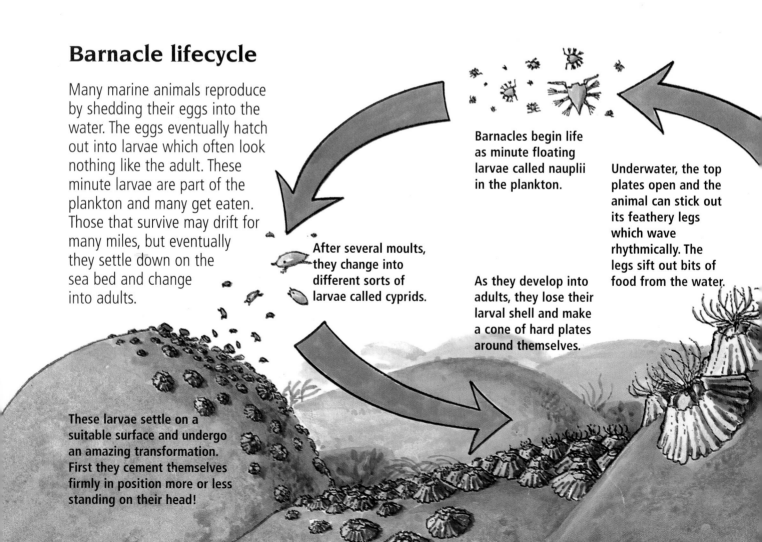

Barnacles begin life as minute floating larvae called nauplii in the plankton.

After several moults, they change into different sorts of larvae called cyprids.

Underwater, the top plates open and the animal can stick out its feathery legs which wave rhythmically. The legs sift out bits of food from the water.

As they develop into adults, they lose their larval shell and make a cone of hard plates around themselves.

These larvae settle on a suitable surface and undergo an amazing transformation. First they cement themselves firmly in position more or less standing on their head!

Plankton

Floating around in the water are millions of tiny plants and animals called plankton. Many can only be seen with a powerful magnifying glass or under a microscope. They are very important because the plankton plants can make their own food, using energy from sunlight, just like plants on land. Then the plankton animals can eat the plankton plants. The small animals are eaten by bigger ones and the bigger ones by even bigger ones. This is called a food chain.

Top-of-page picture bands

This book is divided into different saltwater habitats. Each habitat (type of living place) has a different picture band at the top of the page. These are shown below.

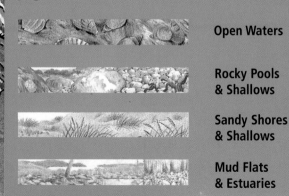

Open Waters

Rocky Pools & Shallows

Sandy Shores & Shallows

Mud Flats & Estuaries

How to use this book

To identify an animal that you don't recognise, like the two animals shown here, follow these steps.

1 **Decide what habitat you are in.** If you're unsure about this, read the descriptions, at the start of each section to see which one fits best. Each habitat has a different picture band heading and these are shown on this page.

2 **Decide what sort of animal it is.** Is it a reptile, a fish or a mollusc, or something else entirely? Look at the descriptions on pages 6–7 to find out. For example, the Mantis Shrimp (see below and page 69) is a crustacean (one type of animal with a shell).

4 **If you can't find the animal there**, look through the other sections. Animals move around, and you may see them in more than one habitat. You will find the animal above is a Sea Hare (see page 36).

5 **If you still can't find the animal**, you may need to look in a larger field guide. You may have spotted a very rare creature!

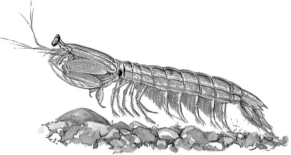

3 **Look through the pages of animals with your habitat picture band at the top.** The picture and information given for each animal will help you to identify it.

What Could I See?

Animals that live in the sea and on the seashore do not always look like animals. Instead of having legs and moving around grazing or searching for prey, many marine animals stay firmly fixed to rocks looking just like plants!

Fish

Fish have different numbers of fins on their backs. Look out for the number of back fins and how close they are to each other. One, two or three fins are usual.

Eels have one long fin

Herrings have one short fin

Wrasse have one long fin, spiny in front and soft at the back

Gobies have two fins, close together

Bib and cod have three fins

Crustaceans

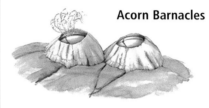

Acorn Barnacles

Edible Crab

Sand Hoppers

Isopod

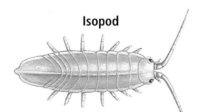

Crabs, lobsters, shrimps, prawns, sand hoppers and isopods belong to this group. They have a hard, plated skin and many pairs of jointed limbs. As they grow, they must moult (shed their skin) and grow a bigger one. Look out for empty crab shells.

Molluscs

Most animals with shells are molluscs. If they have one shell they are called sea snails or gastropods. Those with two hinged shells are called bivalves. Barnacles also have shells, but they are crustaceans like crabs and lobsters. Molluscs also include the cuttlefish and chitons.

Smooth Periwinkle

Mussel

Little Cuttlefish

Chiton

Echinoderms

Starfish, brittle stars, urchins, and sea cucumbers belong to this group. All except sea cucumbers have many long or short spines. Most starfish have five arms, but some have more, so count their arms.

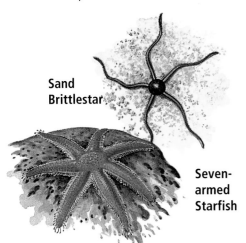

Sand Brittlestar

Seven-armed Starfish

Slate-pencil Sea Urchin

Other attached animals

Star Sea Squirts have a sac-like body with two openings (siphons) out of which water squirts if the body is pressed. Sponges come in many shapes and colours. They suck in water through tiny holes all over them. The water comes out again through a few larger holes.

Star Sea Squirt

Bath Sponge

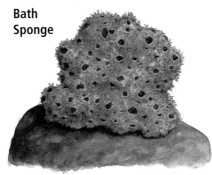

Is it a plant?

Seaweeds do not have flowers. So anything flower-like is likely to be an animal! They may be anemones, hydroids (sea firs), bryozoans, soft corals or hard corals. Use a magnifying lens to look for minute anemone-like heads on any bushy, twiggy, tree or fern-like growths.

Parasitic Anemone

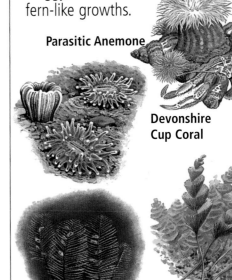

Devonshire Cup Coral

Feather Hydroid

Spiral-tufted Bryzoan

Worms & worm-like animals

Spiral Tube Worm

Look for the different shapes of tube worms. The animal will only stick its head and tentacles out when it is underwater. Worms that do not live in tubes either have smooth bodies or are divided up into lots of segments.

Paddle Worm

Open Water

A single sailor miles from land, must feel very lonely at times. But, if he had eyes like microscopes, he would see that he had millions of companions. Sea water is like a soup filled with tiny floating animals and plants called plankton.

When the weather is very calm and warm, you might see these as patches of colour floating on the surface. At night they may show up as bright flashes of phosphorescence.

Many larger sea creatures also live in the open ocean. Animals such as turtles, basking sharks and many other fish, spend their whole lives wandering the seas in search of food. Some make very long journeys migrating thousands of miles, while others have a relatively small 'home patch'.

If you are lucky, you will see these when you are travelling on a ship or out in a boat on holiday. You might also see whales, dolphins and seals. With a good pair of binoculars, you can make some exciting finds from a cliff top or other such vantage point.

Most fish can swim strongly and go where they like. Jellyfish and many tiny planktonic animals can swim down or up, but are swept along sideways by tidal currents. Some have floats or sails and are blown along by winds – in rough weather they may get blown ashore and stranded. This picture shows thirteen animals from this book; see how many you can identify.

Plankton (in circle), Anchovy, Cod, Flying Fish, Sea Gooseberries, Herring, Compass Jellyfish, Moon Jellyfish, Portuguese Man-of-war, Rhyzostoma Jellyfish, Mackerel, Basking Shark, Loggerhead Turtle.

Loggerhead Turtle

This turtle is an unusual find. If you do see this or a leatherback, report your sighting to the Natural History Museum, London, or the nearest marine biological station. Most of those seen around the shores are young or half-grown turtles that have been stranded and may be lying dead on beaches. They feed on crabs, shellfish, sea urchins and jellyfish. Large specimens are often covered with Goose Barnacles which have settled on them out of the plankton.

Size: Up to 1 m
Where to look: Chance encounters only
Range: An ocean wanderer

Caretta caretta

Leatherback Turtle

You may be fortunate enough to see one of these huge turtles from a boat, especially from June to September. It feeds mainly on jellyfish (even those with powerful stings). Leatherback Turtles sometimes get entangled in fishermen's nets or crab-pot ropes. Sometimes they swallow floating plastic, thinking that it is a jellyfish; this may kill them eventually.

Size: Up to 2 m; weighing over 400 kg
Where to look: Chance encounters only
Range: An ocean wanderer

Dermochelys coriacea

Basking Shark

Cetorhinus maximus

This huge shark often swims close to the shore, especially in summer. With its enormous mouth wide open, it swims slowly along channelling in water rich in plankton, its source of food. The water passes out through its gills which are lined with 'gill rakers' which sift out the plankton.

Basking Sharks give birth to living young, having carried them for about two years – there is still a lot to learn about their lives.
Size: Up to 12 m long
Where to look: In summer look down from clifftops, headlands or from boats; not common
Range: Widely distributed in summer; winter spent in deeper water

Flying Fish

This fish has evolved broad front (pectoral) fins. It propels itself up and out of the water with its tail and uses the fins to glide and so to escape from predators. In 'flight', Flying Fish may cover up to 90 metres and stay in the air for eight to ten seconds. There are two-winged and four-winged groups, the latter being much more skilful 'fliers'.
Size: Up to 30 cm
Where to look: In summer at sea from an open boat
Range: Mediterranean; summer visitor to northern waters

Exocoetus volitans

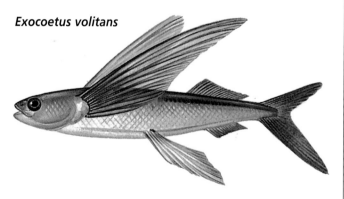

John Dory

According to legend, St Peter held this fish in order to take a gold coin from its mouth. The dark spot is said to be the imprint of the saint's thumb, encircled with gold. The John Dory feeds on small fish which it stalks very slowly. When close enough, it shoots out its jaws to form a sort of tunnel and the fish is seized and swallowed. It is a highly prized edible fish.
Size: Up to about 35 cm, more rarely 60 cm
Where to look: Often seen by divers and snorkellers in summer
Range: European waters south of Scotland

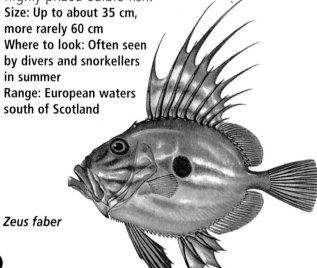

Zeus faber

Fish

Cod

The Cod is an amazing egg-layer. One small Cod may lay up to a quarter of a million eggs, and a large Cod as many as five million. Yet comparatively few survive to adulthood. Those that do can live up to twenty years.

Cod prefer cold waters of about 5°C, as deep as 500 metres. They migrate long distances especially in the Barents Sea of the Arctic.

Size: Up to 1.5 m; weighing up to 35 kg but most large ones have been fished out
Where to look: Young close inshore, sometimes in rock pools
Range: European waters north of Spain

Gadus morrhua

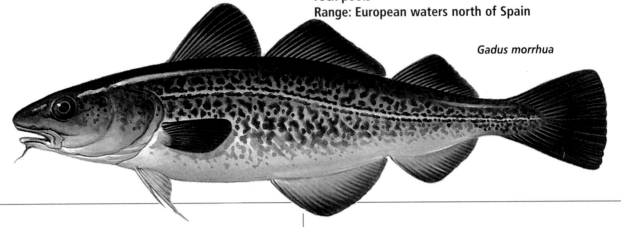

Pollack

In summer and autumn, you may see many of these fish in their first year and about five centimetres long swimming around harbour walls. The Pollack is a species often caught by anglers fishing around wrecks. The adults feed on sand eels, prawns and small squid. In summer, shoals often swim into estuaries.

Size: Up to about 1 m; weighing up to 10 kg
Where to look: In clear water around harbour and pier walls
Range: Throughout European waters

Pollachius pollachius

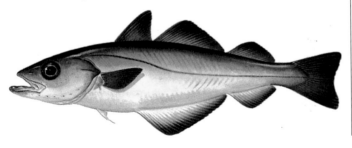

Bib

This smallish species, also called the Pouting, is often caught by anglers fishing from piers, harbour walls and jetties. It is common in small shoals over sandy bottoms and rocky places. There it feeds on shrimps and other small crustaceans, molluscs and little fish. Its beautiful golden copper colour with darker stripes and a small barbel make identification easy.

Size: Up to 25 cm; inshore ones usually smaller
Where to look: Look down in clear water from piers and harbour walls; divers and snorkellers will see them around wrecks
Range: European waters north to southern Norway

Trisopterus luscus

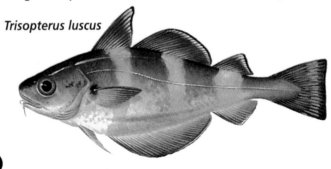

Anchovy

Looking like a smaller and slimmer Herring, the Anchovy is another plankton feeder. In summer, they sometimes migrate into estuaries and inshore waters. They are a favourite seafood in Russia, Italy and Spain. In the North Sea, the Anchovy has been subject to over-fishing. The female may lay as may as 20,000 eggs in a sort of mat on the sea-bed.

Size: Average about 10 cm
Where to look: Can be attracted with lights to boats and piers at night
Range: Throughout European waters

Engraulis encrasicolus

Herring

Herring are plankton feeders and they swim in enormous shoals off Europe's northern coasts. A female may lay up to 45,000 eggs when she is three years old. Herring is a species that has been over-fished because of its popularity as a seafood. They tend to swim in places where the warm Gulf Stream currents mix with cold Arctic waters.

Size: Up to 40 cm
Where to look: Comes to the surface at night and may be seen from boats and piers by torchlight
Range: Northern European waters

Clupea harengus

Mackerel

The Mackerel is a migrant fish that feeds inshore from May to October. Shoals winter in the Hurd Deep off the English Channel and in deep water off the Continental Shelf, before moving inshore to spawn in spring. A fast-swimming fish, the Mackerel feeds on Sandeels, small fish and shrimps. Mackerel are now heavily over-fished.

Size: Average up to 40 cm
Where to look: In summer watch for shoals breaking surface; easily caught by angling from piers
Range: Throughout European waters

Scomber scombrus

Floating Animals

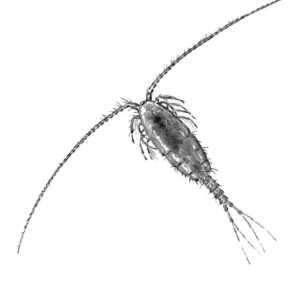

Cyclops species

Copepod

In spring, use a plankton net (you can buy one from an aquarium shop) from a pier or jetty or from a boat. Remember copepods are minute and you will only see them as specks in your jar. They feed on diatoms and there are a great many different species. It has been said there are more copepods in the world than all other multicellular animals put together. They form an important food species for vast numbers of baby fish and larvae of sea life.

Size: Larger species about the size of a grain of rice
Where to look: Surface of the sea
Range: Worldwide

Marine Plankton

Plankton is the name given to the millions of tiny creatures which float and drift in the sea's currents. Use your plankton net and you will catch a great variety of them. Transfer the catch from the jar in the end of your net to a clean jar of seawater. Light it with your torch from behind or hold the jar against the sun. Some plankton are young stages of crustaceans, worms, sea snails and a host of other creatures. Others live their whole lives as plankton. With your hand lens, you will discover a whole new world of fantastic shapes and beauty.

Size: From pin's head to grain of rice
Where to look: Surface waters of the sea
Range: Worldwide

Sea Gooseberry

This animal is also known as Comb Jelly. If you catch some in your plankton net, put them into clear seawater in a small aquarium and watch how they swim. Their trailing tentacles contain lasso cells covered in sticky knobs. These trap planktonic animals, which are then passed to the mouth. Look closely with your hand lens and you may see beautiful iridescent colours rippling over the animal. This is caused by the beating of many rows of tiny hairs. These are the 'combs' that move it along.

Size: About 1 cm across
Where to look: Surface waters of the sea: sometimes washed a up on shore
Range: Throughout European waters

Pleurobrachia pileus

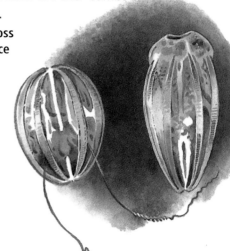

Moon Jellyfish

These are the commonest summer jellyfish, often coming close to shore in large shoals. Luckily, they do not usually sting. Like most jellyfish, about ninety per cent of the Moon Jellyfish's body weight is water, so as soon as it strands itself on a beach it begins to dry out and die. Watch how it swims by pulsing its body. They are often eaten by the Lion's Mane Jellyfish (see page 16). The four mauve rings contain eggs if the jellyfish is female and fertilizing fluid if it is male. They are a useful identification feature.

Size: Average about 12 cm; large ones up to 25 cm
Where to look: From boats in summer or stranded at the tide's edge
Range: Worldwide

Aurelia aurita

Compass Jellyfish

It has twenty-four long, trailing tentacles which, unlike the Moon Jellyfish, will sting you, so **do not touch it**. Normally the Compass Jellyfish uses these stings to capture small fish for food. As it is not common, you will need patience to see one as it pulses its way through the sea. Unlike the Moon Jellyfish, the Compass Jellyfish is a 'hermaphrodite', which means that it is both male and female. When disturbed this jellyfish sometimes glows with luminescence.

Size: Up to 30 cm
Where to look: Look into clear sea from piers, promenades, jetties or boats
Range: Throughout European waters

Chrysaora hysoscella

Jellyfish (Rhizostoma)

This is one of the largest jellyfish you will see and it is quite harmless. It has a firm white body or bell and no long tentacles. Underneath it hangs a bunch of 'arms' looking rather like a sprig of cauliflower. These are covered in tiny openings into which plankton can be sucked and passed along channels into the mouth and stomach. In some years, large numbers are blown ashore and die.

Size: Up to 80 cm across and almost as deep
Where to look: Look down from piers, cliffs and boats; sometimes stranded
Range: Most European waters

Rhizostoma pulmo

Jellyfish (Pelagia)

This is a pink-spotted, mushroom-shaped jellyfish. Normally a resident of sub-tropical seas, in some years these jellyfish drift northwards to northern European coasts. They glow in the sea at night with a greenish luminescence. Although this jellyfish is beautiful, **do not touch it** for it can sting. The real purpose of these stings is to paralyze the creatures it catches for food.

Size: Fully grown about 10 cm
Where to look: Chance encounters; more common in some years than others
Range: Throughout European waters

Pelagia noctiluca

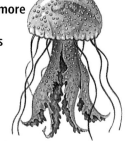

Floating Animals

Lion's Mane Jellyfish

Do not touch this huge jellyfish. It is the largest jellyfish known and it gives a very unpleasant sting. It comes in several different colours. One species is coloured in shades of brown to deep red. A less common species ranges from blue to purple. It trails a mass of thin stinging tentacles up to 8 metres long! As it swims through the sea, these spread like a net to capture prey. If you snare one of these animals in your plankton net, tip it out and thoroughly rinse your net without touching it.

Size: Occasionally up to 2 m; usually up to 30 cm
Where to look: Look down from piers, jetties or boats in summer seas
Range: Northern European waters

Cyanea Capillata

Portuguese Man-of-War

This is not a true jellyfish but it stings like one, so **do not touch it**! The powerful stinging tentacles may extend for several metres. It drifts on the sea's surface, held there by its large blue air bladder. The diagonally raised part of this acts like a yacht's sail to catch the wind. Every so often, this creature keeps itself wet by rolling sideways. There is one fish that can live among its tentacles without being stung!

Size: Up to about 25 cm
Where to look: Chance encounters; in some years, they drift ashore in numbers in summer
Range: Most common off coasts of southern Europe

Physalia physalis

String Jelly

This strange animal looks like a piece of ragged string trailing in the water. The 'string' is a collection of tiny, individual, bell-shaped animals. Some of these have a single tentacle and catch food for the colony. Others produce eggs and sperm. A small float at the end of the 'string' keeps the colony in the surface waters.

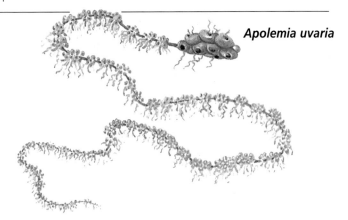

Apolemia uvaria

Size: Up to 20 m long!
Where to look: Floating in surface waters
Range: Mediterranean; drifts north to British Isles in some years

By-the-wind Sailor

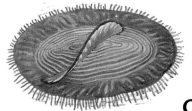

As a seashore explorer, you will sometimes discover a creature that has come from a faraway sea. This is one such species. It lives on the sea surface, driven to and fro by the winds, and sometimes it is blown ashore. It looks like a miniature oval raft with a translucent sail set at an angle across the top. Trailing beneath it are the short 'tentacles' that capture food.

Size: Up to 8 cm long
Where to look: Occasionally seen from boats and piers; chance encounters after an onshore wind strands it
Range: Worldwide but much commoner in warm waters

Velella velella

Violet Sea Snail

This lovely sea snail floats on the sea's surface by secreting a raft of bubbles which support it. To keep it even more buoyant, its shell is extremely thin. Violet Sea Snails seem to live in shoals together with By-the-wind Sailors, on which they feed. A single Violet Sea Snail will slowly consume a By-the-wind Sailor and leave only the horny float.

Size: Up to about 1.5 cm
Where to look: Seashores for stranded and empty shells; more common in some years than others
Range: European waters but not often seen

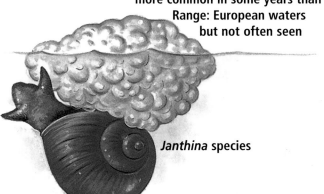

Janthina species

Common Salp

Salps look like small, transparent barrels made of firm jelly. They are in fact, swimming sea squirts with an opening at each end of the 'barrel'. They can swim by squirting water out of one end but they mostly drift in water currents. At certain times of year, long chains of individuals are formed by budding. A new individual grows out from one end but stays attached to the first one. Then another grows and so on; they eventually split up into separate individuals.

Size: Individuals up to 2.5 cm; chains up to about 10 cm
Where to look: Surface waters, sometimes so many you can't swim between them. Mostly in September/October in British waters.
Range: Mediterranean and warm waters; carried to northern European waters each summer but does not survive winter there.

Salpa fusiformis

Blue Buttons

This animal is closely related to the By-the-wind Sailor, but as you can see, it lacks a sail. It is an ocean drifter and is only occasionally blown ashore. They usually appear in shoals on the sea's surface. Like the By-the-wind Sailor, this is actually a colony (collection of individuals), some of which form the float while others feed, defend or reproduce.

Size: Disc up to 8 cm
Where to look: Chance encounters when drifted inshore, or seen from a boat
Range: Mostly Mediterranean and southern waters

Porpita species

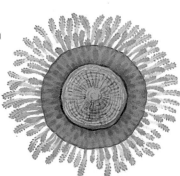

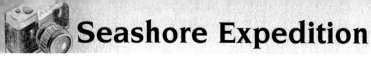

Seashore Expedition

Next time you go to the beach, why not turn your visit into an expedition. There is so much to see and do if you have the right clothing and equipment.

Although it may be warm inland, there may be a cold wind on the beach. However, being out in the sun beside the sea can easily lead to sunburn even if it feels cold. So wear a sun-hat, sun-cream and a T-shirt, and take a tracksuit in case it turns cold.

What to take

The following equipment will help you find, see, examine and record shore animals.

1 **Trowel** for digging up burrowing animals on sandy and muddy shores.
2 **Old kitchen sieve** for washing out buried animals in sand and mud.
3 **Long-handled net** for catching animals in rock pools or along the water's edge.
4 **'Goggle-box' or face mask** to help you look in rock pools (see pages 44–45).
5 **Plastic bucket**, with a lid for carrying live animals to a comfortable spot to look at them.
6 **Magnifying glass:** A small folding glass with a magnification of x10 is excellent. Wear it on a string around your neck.
7 **Plastic bags** for collecting seaweeds and shells.
8 **Field notebook with pencils and biros** to make notes and records.
9 **Camera**, to record where you have been and what you found.
10 **Light backpack** to carry everything leaving your hands free for scrambling over rocks.

If you are stung

If you are badly stung and feel ill, or if you usually react badly to stings, you should see a doctor. These simple First Aid treatments will help to stop the pain.

• **Fish stings:** These can be very painful. As soon as you can, put your foot or wherever the sting was, into a bowl of water as hot as you can bear. Leave it in until it stops hurting.
• **Jellyfish stings:** Pour vinegar over the sting to prevent further stings, then pick any bits of tentacle off using tweezers or gloves. Fresh water may cause any bits of tentacle sticking to you to sting some more.
• **Sea urchin spines:** If the spines stick a long way into you and break off, they are difficult to get out and you should see a doctor. Hot water or local anaesthetic ointments will help to stop the pain until you get there.
• **Worm bristles:** If you get small bristles in your hands from animals like bristle worms, you can sometimes get them out by laying Elastoplast over them and then pulling it off.

Making a record

Your notes will help you to remember what you have seen. If you visit the same beach regularly, you can build up a picture of how things change with the seasons. You can also compare beaches.

1 **Buy a small waterproof notebook** or make your own from plasticized paper (get this from an art shop or a good stationers).

2 **Or make a simple writing board** from white Formica. Write on it in pencil and copy your notes out later on paper.
3 **Give your beach a name.** Each time you visit it, record the date, what the weather was and where the tide was.
4 **Write down where you found each animal** – in a rock pool, on a boulder, on a mud flat. What was it doing? Were there lots of others on the shore or only a few?

Where to look

Animals that live on the seashore need to stay wet while the tide is out. Many animals take shelter under rocks and stones where there is likely to be a small puddle of water. This is the best place to look for small crabs, little stars, and worms.

After searching it is very important to gently turn stones back the way you found them. Sea creatures will soon die if left in the open. The best time to visit a rocky shore is an hour or two before low tide. Animals that live near low tide level include many anemones, sea squirts, flatworms, etc. They have soft bodies and no shells and would soon dry out if they lived further up the beach.

• Which animals can only live down near the sea?
• Which can survive near the top of the beach?

Another good place to search is off the sides of floating pontoons. Get permission first, then lie flat on your stomach and look over the side. You should see crabs, shrimps and small fish. Try pushing your net through the seaweed and see what you catch.

The SPLASH ZONE is wetted by spray at high tide, but is only covered when storms drive waves on to the beach.

The MIDDLE ZONE is the largest area. It is always uncovered at low tide.

The UPPER ZONE is often uncovered even at high tide.

The LOWER ZONE is only uncovered by the lowest tides.

The SHALLOW WATER ZONE is always covered by water even at low tide.

Rock Pools & Shallows

The European coastline has many rocky shores, especially in northern areas. Such shores are very rewarding places to look for sea creatures. There are plenty of holes and crevices for animals to hide in and a good foothold for those that spend their lives clinging to rocks.

One of the first things you might notice, especially on Atlantic shores, is a thick cover of slippery seaweeds. These provide homes and food to yet more animals.

Life on the shore is not easy. When the tide is out, the animals have to find ways of staying damp especially on hot sunny days. In rough weather, they are pounded by waves as the tide comes back in. Deep rock pools solve some of these problems and provide excellent homes for many animals.

Some rocky shores such as those in sea lochs, are sheltered from rough weather and waves. You will find that the sorts of animals and the numbers of them are different on sheltered and exposed shores.

The Mediterranean Sea is almost cut off from the Atlantic Ocean and is only joined to it by the narrow Straits of Gibraltar. Tides here are very small and the water only drops by about half a metre – so there is only a very narrow seashore. If you want to see marine creatures here, you will have to wade, swim or better still, snorkel with a face mask. This picture shows nineteen animals from this book; see how many you can identify.

Beadlet Anemone, Dahlia Anemone, Gem Anemone, Snakelocks Anemone, Butterfish, Chiton, Devonshire Cup Coral, Edible Crab, Sea Lemon, Limpet, Mussel, Common Periwinkle, Sea Slug, Star Sea Squirt, Common Sea Urchin, Sea Scorpion, Breadcrumb Sponge, Purse Sponge, Keel Worm.

Fish

Tompot Blenny

One of the prettiest and most inquisitive of the blennies, the Tompot lives mainly just below low tide level. Crabbers sometimes catch them in their crab-pots. If you are fortunate enough to get one, you will find it makes an ideal aquarium inhabitant. Put a smallish pot or a jar made from dark glass in the aquarium with it, and it will spend much of its time watching you from inside the opening.

Size: Up to 15 cm long
Where to look: In shallows below low tide; in holes and crevices
Range: Most European coasts as far north as Scotland. Not in the North Sea

Parablennius gattorugine

Shanny

Like all blennies, the Shanny has thick lips and eyes set high up on its head, giving it a comical look. It is common and easily caught with a push net. You will find it a perfect aquarium fish as it quickly becomes 'tame'. Put a large stone in mid-tank so that it comes above water level. After dark, you will find the blennies resting there, partly out of the water.

Size: Average 8 cm; up to 16 cm
Where to look: In rock pools and beneath large rocks on the shore; use your goggle-box (page 44) to see young ones
Range: Most common on north European coasts south to Portugal

Lipophrys pholis

Montagu's Blenny

This blenny might be confused with the Tompot, so look carefully at the two pictures. Unlike the Tompot, this species is found in rock pools on the shore. The male prepares a scooped-out sand nest for the female to lay her eggs in. He then stays on guard. You may catch a Montagu's Blenny when pushing your net through rock pool seaweeds.

Size: Up to 8 cm
Where to look: Rock pools
Range: Mediterranean and southern waters to south-west Britain

Coryphoblennius galerita

Rock Goby

If you search under seaweed and beneath rocks near low tide you will almost certainly find a Rock Goby. As soon as you expose one, it will jump and skid away into hiding. They will live in aquariums but are very nervous and tend to hide away. At first quick glance, you could confuse this fish with a blenny, but blennies have one continuous dorsal fin, while the Rock Gory has two dorsal fins. Look for a yellow or orange band at the top of the first dorsal fin.

Size: Average about 6–8 cm, but up to 12 cm
Where to look: Under seaweed and rocks on lower rocky shore
Range: European coasts, north to Scotland

Gobius paganellus

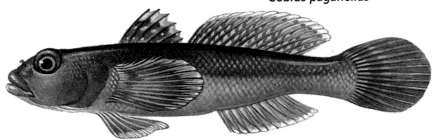

Two-spot Goby

You may be lucky to find a small shoal of these gobies swimming in a deep rock pool. Look for them after many days of calm, summer seas. If they are there, you will always find them swimming in mid-water and not on the bottom. They are very difficult to catch, as they move like lightning when disturbed. Note the position of the two spots.

Size: Mostly about 5–6 cm
Where to look: Rock pools; can also be seen amongst tall seaweeds when snorkelling
Range: Most European coasts

Gobiusculus flavescens

Butterfish

If you spot one of these slippery little fish as you turn over a rock you will see how quickly it wriggles away to cover. The dark spots below its dorsal fin plainly tell you that it is a Butterfish. The female lays eggs between stones or in an empty shell between December and March. Both parents take turns at guarding them sometimes wrapping their bodies around the egg mass.

Size: Average 15–20 cm
Where to look: Rocky shores under rocks; amongst seaweed and in pools
Range: English Channel northwards

Pholis gunnellus

Clingfish

Also called the Suckerfish, this fish's flattish body has a large sucker disc which it uses to grip on to a rocky surface. In this way, it resists the force of currents and tidal movements. In summer, the female lays a batch of eggs on a stone and both parents guard them. Clingfish are interesting aquarium fish as they cling to the glass sides.

Size: Up to 5 cm
Where to look: Middle to lower shore under rocks in pools; not easy to find
Range: European coasts north to Scotland

Lepadogaster lepadogaster

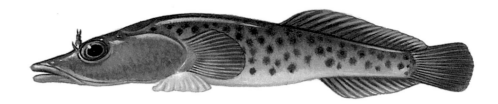

Worm Pipefish

You may find this common little pipefish sheltering in the shallow water under a stone on the lower shore. If you do, put it out in more open water and watch how it swims. Its eggs are 'glued' into a shallow groove along the belly of the male after they are laid by the female. Do not try to keep one of these fish in an aquarium because it is impossible for you to provide all the tiny copepods they need for food.

Size: Up to 14 cm
Where to look: Under rocks and among seaweed in rock pools
Range: Northern European coasts

Nerophis lumbriciformis

Five Bearded Rockling

Rocklings are easy fish to recognize. Look for the barbels (whiskers) around the mouth which help them to find food. Look also at the two back fins. The first one has one long ray followed by a fringe of very short rays set in a groove. Young rocklings live near the water surface. They are called 'mackerel midge' and are eaten by birds such as terns and puffins. You may also find other members of the rockling family which only have three or four barbels.

Size: Up to 20 cm
Where to look: Rock pools; sometimes under rocks
Range: Northern European coasts

Ciliata mustela

Damsel Fish

This species is very common along the Mediterranean coast. Although fairly large, it eats only small plankton. Adults are dark brown with paler centres to the scales, while the young are bluish violet. Males take up territory along with many others and settle down less than twenty centimetres from each other. Each male guards a stone on which the female deposits her eggs. This fish makes an interesting aquarium fish.

Size: Mostly about 10 cm
Where to look: Sea-grass (*Zostera*) beds, rocky shore and harbour walls; often seen when snorkelling
Range: Mediterranean

Chromis chromis

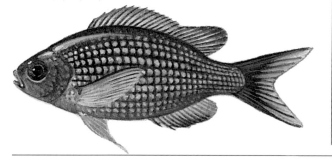

Sea Scorpion

This prickly fish is beautifully camouflaged with green, black, yellow and orange shades. It can slowly change colour to match its background. Sea Scorpions will hide and then rush out and seize even quite large prey in their very large mouths. Their food is mainly small crustaceans such as crabs, prawns and also the occasional small fish. They always show a preference for moving food.

Size: Up to about 20 cm
Where to look: Rock pools, often under rocks
Range: Northern European coasts

Taurulus bubalis

Scorpion Fish

Do not handle these fish, as they have sharp, poisonous spines. If you are stung, soak the sting thoroughly with very hot water. When disturbed, the Scorpion Fish enlarges its head by swelling out its spiny gill covers. This makes other fish avoid catching it for food. Scorpion Fish hide behind seaweed curtains and rocks, and suddenly dart out to seize passing prey. Even their eyes are camouflaged.

Size: Average adult about 15 cm
Where to look: Rock pools but well camouflaged
Range: Mediterranean and north to Biscay

Scorpaena porcus

Fish

Corkwing Wrasse

This is the wrasse you are most likely to see in rock pools. Females are mostly a dark mottled brown, whilst the males are brighter with iridescent blue bars on the head. A useful aid to identification is a black spot at the base of the tail and another less clear one behind the eye. The male builds a nest by stuffing a rock crevice with seaweeds. He stays on guard after the female has entered and laid her eggs. Sometimes corkwings will act as a cleaner fish picking parasites off larger fish.

Size: Up to 15 cm, sometimes to 25 cm
Where to look: Rock pools with plenty of seaweed
Range: Most European coasts

Crenilabrus melops

Ballan Wrasse

The Ballan is the largest of the common European wrasse. It may also be the oldest since it lives for at least twenty-five years. It is very variable in colour but most are a mottled green, brown or reddish colour with paler spots on the fins. Like all wrasse, it has thick lips and one long back fin. Watch the way it swims, by 'rowing' with its front fins. At night, the Ballan goes to sleep after wedging itself safely in a crevice. These fish are so dozy that divers can sometimes pick them up! Ballan have strong teeth, some in their throat, to crush the shellfish, crabs and prawns on which they feed.

Size: Up to 40 cm, rarely 60 cm
Where to look: Emerald green young in
rock pools in late summer
Range: Most European coasts; rare in Mediterranean

Labrus bergylta

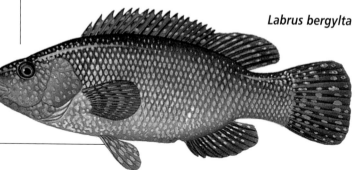

Lumpsucker

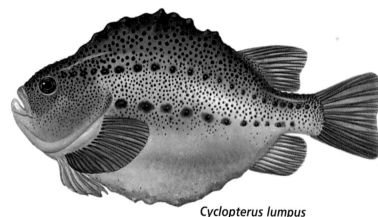

Cyclopterus lumpus

Even small lumpsuckers can be recognized from the hard, bony lumps on their fat bodies. They also have a large sucker underneath, with which they cling tightly to rocks. Even large waves do not wash them off. Lumpsuckers can live down to 200 metres but in spring they come into shallow water and on to the shore, to lay their eggs. The eggs are guarded by the male. When they hatch, the young find food and shelter among seaweeds.

Size: Up to 50 cm
Where to look: Deep rock pools
Washed ashore after severe spring storms
Range: Northern European waters, south to Portugal

Fifteen-spined Stickleback

Look out for the spines on the back and the long thin tail. The male gathers scraps of seaweeds and builds a nest among longer seaweeds. He then swims tightly around the nest, trailing a long filament and binding the seaweed into a hollow ball. The filament is a secretion from his kidneys. The female later lays her eggs inside and leaves them to be guarded by the male. This species feeds on tiny crustaceans, especially copepods.

Size: Average about 15 cm
Where to look: In summer in low tide rock pools
Range: Biscay (south France) northwards

Spinachia spinachia

Dogfish

Nocturnal hunters, these small inshore sharks feed on any small animals they can find on the seabed. The females lay their eggs in capsules and attach them to seaweeds by means of long twisting tendrils. For up to eleven months, the tiny Dogfish feeds on its yolk sac and finally bursts out of the capsule to swim free in the sea. To fertilize the eggs, the male wraps himself around the female and injects his sperm into her body.

Size: Up to 60 cm, sometimes 1 m
Where to look: The egg capsules (mermaids' purses) are often washed ashore. Look for adults in shallow harbours, off jetty walls, etc. They are great scavengers
Range: Throughout European waters

Scyliorhinus canicula

Size: Up to 2.75 m
Where to look: You will probably have to snorkel to see these fish, or visit an aquarium
Range: Most European waters;
similar Moray eel found in Mediterranean

Conger conger

Conger Eel

These are great hunters of cuttlefish, fish, crabs and lobsters, and they have very powerful jaws which can shut like a trap. They live among rocks and in wrecks, usually in cracks and holes with only their heads sticking out. An adult Conger may lay up to six million eggs, but does so only once in its life. Their bodies are scaleless and covered with slippery slime.

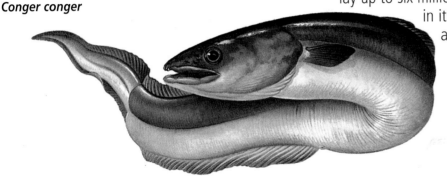

On the Rocks

Seaweeds are the plants of the sea. Just like land plants, they need light to grow and so are only found on the seashore and in shallow water. They do not need roots because there is water all round them. Instead they have a 'holdfast' which fixes them firmly to the rocks.

There are three main groups called reds, greens and browns depending on what colour pigments they contain. They range in size from the huge brown kelps many metres long, to delicate red seaweeds only a few centimetres high.

Studying kelp

At very low tides, the large brown kelp seaweeds may be exposed. These have a large strong, tangled holdfast to fix them firmly to the rock. The spaces between the branches of the holdfast make an ideal home for tiny shore animals. Up to 300 have been found in one holdfast. Don't try pulling these long-lived seaweeds off the rocks. Instead, get out your magnifying glass and see what you can find. **Watch out for incoming tides.**

Seaweed homes

Many animals use seaweed as a hideaway and a place to live. You can find out which ones by 'washing' some seaweed.

1 **Collect a bunch of bushy seaweeds.** Put them straight into a bag so nothing is lost. Do not take too much seaweed.

2 **Put the seaweed into a large bowl** or bucket of sea water. Carefully shake and wash it.

3 **Take the seaweed out and see what animals** have dropped off. You should find lots of small sea snails, shrimps and sea spiders in your bowl.

4 **Try washing long weeds in a bucket** without pulling them off the rocks. Some animals attach themselves firmly to the stems and fronds of large seaweeds. Look for attached and plant-like animals like sea firs and sea mats.

Pressing seaweeds

Delicate red and green seaweeds make beautiful patterns when pressed and dried, but brown seaweeds are often too bulky to press well. Here is what to do:

1 **Float the seaweed in a dish of water.** Slip paper under the seaweed.
2 **Spread the seaweed fronds (branches)** out with your paintbrush.

3 **Gently slide the paper out of the water** leaving the seaweed neatly spread out on it. Tip the tray to help drain the water off.

4 **Lay the wet paper down on several sheets of newspaper.** Cover the seaweed with gauze (nappy liners), then with newspaper. Press using heavy books.

5 **Change the newspaper the next day and a few days after.** In a week, it should be dry and the seaweed will be stuck firmly to the paper.
6 **Store your seaweed papers** in plastic wallets in a loose-leaf file. If you label your papers in pencil before you start, you can build up a collection of seaweeds from different areas.

Wandering limpets

Some animals with shells can close up when the tide is out and keep their own little pool of water inside their shell. This is how limpets, barnacles, mussels and some snails manage to live out in the open on the tops of the rocks.

Limpets cling so tightly to the rock that they eventually make circular grooves in the surface. When the tide is in they move slowly over the rocks, but return to their home spot as the tide goes down. Look for rings on the rock where a limpet used to live. Look also for semi-circular patterns of tiny scratch marks made by the limpet's hard, rough tongue scraping food off the rocks.

Don't try to kick limpets off their rocks. You will damage them and they will die within a day or two.

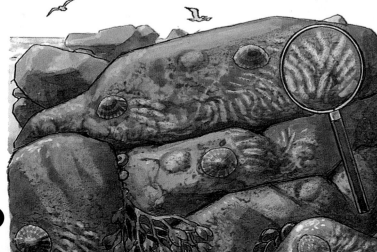

Attached Animals

Star Sea Squirt

It is difficult to tell that this is a Sea Squirt. This is because many tiny individuals grow together in a colony. They are arranged in vividly coloured star-shaped patterns embedded in a firm jelly-like layer. Water is sucked in by each individual and goes out again through the centre of each 'star'. Shades of yellow, blue, green, white and brown are all common.

Size: Variable patches up to about 1 cm thick
Where to look: On damp rocks and bases of large seaweeds near low tide level
Range: Most European coasts

Botryllus schlosseri

Blood Drop Sea Squirt

These small red sea squirts are easy to spot because they often grow in large groups. When exposed by the tide, they contract and their siphons may not be easy to see. However, they will squirt you if you gently prod them! Sea Squirts are hermaphrodite. That is, they produce both eggs and sperm. These are shed alternately into the water where the eggs float and develop.

Size: Up to 2 cm high and 1 cm across
Where to look: In damp places low on the shore. Look at the sides of large rocks under curtains of seaweed
Range: Northern European coasts

Dendrodoa grossularia

This species grows as a group of sea Squirts joined at the base. The soft, transparent body has yellow or white lines running down it and outlining the siphons. This makes them look like the inside of a light bulb. Like all sea squirts, each animal has two siphons, one for inflowing water and the other for outflowing. Look closely, and you should soon find some.

Size: About 2.5 cm
Where to look: Harbour walls, rocks and stones on lower shore
Range: Most European coasts

Light-bulb Sea Squirt

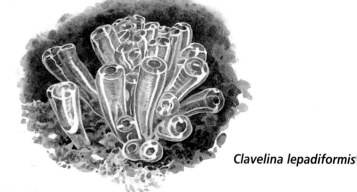

Clavelina lepadiformis

Common Sea Squirt

This delicate-looking sea squirt is soft and quite transparent. If you touch it, it will quickly contract. One siphon is at the top end, the other on its side. In some places, large numbers grow together. Look closely and you will see this creature's internal organs through its transparent skin. It has a short life span of about a year. In order to get enough food, it filters up to 200 litres of water an hour.

Size: Up to 10 cm
Where to look: Pier pilings, harbour walls; sheltered rocks. Especially common in sea lochs
Range: Most European coasts

Ciona intestinalis

Black Sea Cucumber or Cotton Spinner

Surprisingly sausage-shaped, this animal is related to sea urchins. Around the sea cucumber's mouth, short tentacles shovel mud into its digestive system. If continually disturbed, it turns until its rear end faces the enemy and then fires a series of white sticky threads which can enmesh a crab and immobilise it. This gives it the name Cotton Spinner. Having fixed its enemy, the creature sheds the threads and moves off.

Size: Up to 15 cm
Where to look: Lower shore and shallows on rocky shores or among eel grass (*Zostera*)
Range: Most European coasts

Holothuria forskali

Crevice Sea Cucumbers

These sea cucumbers live in holes and crevices in rocks with only the frilly tentacles showing. Like all sea cucumbers, they have rows of short tube feet along the body. These act like tiny suckers so they can move along and grip on to rocks. Lying well protected, a fringe of ten sticky mouth tentacles collects bits of food. They then turn inwards into the mouth and there they are 'licked' clean.

Size: Average 8–10 cm
Where to look: Lower shore under rocks, in crevices and on rock overhangs
Range: Most European coasts

Cucumaria saxicola

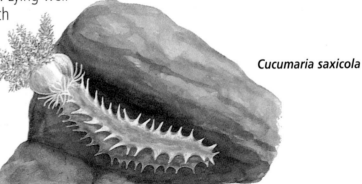

Echinoderms

Edible Sea Urchin

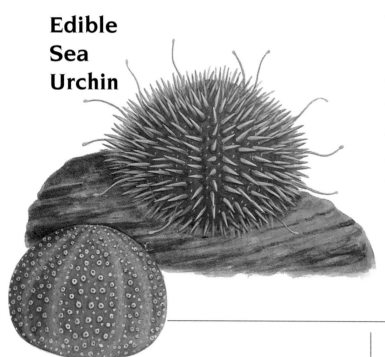

This large urchin has a beautiful pinkish shell (called a 'test') and, sadly, in some areas it has been over-collected for the souvenir trade. The eggs or 'roe' are also eaten. Between its many sharp spines, there are long tube feet. With these, it can climb vertical rocks. If you find one, carefully turn it over and look for a round mouth with five sharp teeth. With these, the urchin browses on seaweeds, sea mats and sea firs. The urchin can live for up to eight years.

Size: Up to 20 cm
Where to look: Lower shore and beyond
Range: European coasts north of Portugal

Echinus esculentus

Green Sea Urchin

Also known as the Shore Sea Urchin, this is a common urchin on many shores. It hides away under rocks and overhangs to avoid predators like the Herring Gull. You will find these urchins under rocks, and they are often covered with pieces of shell and small stones held in place by their tube feet. The strong green spines have purple tips. When you find one, place it in a shallow pool and watch it move about.

Size: Average up to 4 cm
Where to look: Under rocks
Range: Northern European coasts

Psammechinus miliaris

Red Lance Urchin

This type of sea urchin has long, thick, rough spines scattered over its shell (test). There are many small spines between these making it a difficult prey for any gull or large fish. It is a brightly coloured species with a red and yellow body and brown spines with both dark and light bands around them. Like all urchins, this is a herbivore with strong, sharp teeth used for grazing on seaweeds.

Size: Up to 5.5 cm diameter
Where to look: Among rocks, especially where coralline seaweeds grow
Range: Mediterranean, north to Portugal

Stylocidaris affinis

Black Sea Urchins

These black, or very dark, warm water species have quite long spines with sharp tips so be careful when handling them and when swimming over them. Only experts can reliably tell them apart. They usually live in hollows in soft rocks which they have scraped away leaving the rock riddled with holes. Many are collected for the 'roe' which is eaten, and they are disappearing from some areas.

Size: Up to 5 cm across; spines 3 cm
Where to look: Rock pools. Among rocks
when swimming or snorkelling
Range: Mediterranean. *Paracentrotus*
also north to southern Ireland

Arbacia lixula **and** *Paracentrotus lividus*

Spiny Starfish

You can recognize this large, pale starfish from the rows of long spines on the arms. When you find one, look at its amazing structure with your hand lens, especially the ring of tiny pincer-like organs around each spine. It is a great predator on mussels and oysters, which it opens with ease and eats in considerable numbers.

Size: Average about 30 cm, but up to 70 cm in diameter
Where to look: Lower shore among rocks and
seaweed, especially mussel and oyster beds
Range: Throughout European waters

Marthasterias glacialis

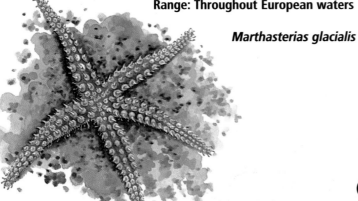

Common Starfish

This very common species is usually yellowish or reddish brown but can be purple. Touch the skin, it will feel rough from the small white spines sticking through the skin. You may find some with only four or even three long arms plus one or two very short ones. Starfish often lose an arm through predator attack or surf damage, but the arms can regrow or 'regenerate'. Common Starfish feed on Mussels and similar shellfish by pulling the shell valves apart, then pushing their stomach into the shell and digesting the body.

Size: Up to 30 cm but mostly average
up to 15 cm
Where to look: Almost anywhere!
Common on Mussel beds
Range: Throughout European
waters except Mediterranean

Asterias rubens

Starfish

The vivid red starfish feeds on sponges, and this is a helpful clue when looking for these creatures. Most female starfish release their eggs into the sea where males fertilize them and larvae result. This species is different. It releases baby starfish directly into the sea. If you keep one in an aquarium, it may release some young.

Size: Up to 20 cm
Where to look: Mostly
on rocks on lower
shore and in
deeper water
Range: Mediterranean
north to Brittany

Echinaster sepositus

Spiny Sun Star

This is one of the most beautiful sun stars, with sometimes as many as fifteen arms covered with spines. It has a crafty way of getting its food. It attacks a Common Starfish (see page 33) and makes it drop off one of its arms. The Spiny Sun Star then begins to eat, gnawing away from the broken end until the whole arm has been eaten.

Size: Up to 35 cm across
Where to look: Lower shores; especially mussel beds where Common Starfish are plentiful
Range: European coasts north of France

Crossaster papposus

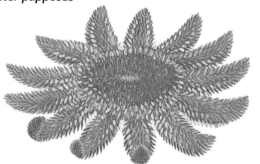

Blood Stars

Blood-red marks on these orange, purple or red starfish give them its name. Unlike most starfish, it broods its young, by protecting them beneath its incurved arms. As soon as the young have grown into perfect stars, they crawl away to lead their own lives. Compare the picture here with that of the Common Starfish (see page 33) and you will notice the Blood Star's arms are thinner, smaller and smooth. It feels very firm when picked up. It feeds almost entirely on sponges.

Size: Up to 10 cm
Where to look: Among large stones and sponge-inhabited places
Range: From Bay of Biscay northwards

Henricia **species**

Starlet

You will have to search carefully to find this small starfish, also called the Cushion Star. It hides away beneath rocks and overhangs. Since it is usually brownish or greenish in colour, it is often not easy to see. Starlets are male for the first couple of years, then become female; their eggs are laid under rocks. Try keeping some in your aquarium, as they settle down well. They eat small shellfish, sea squirts and sponges.

Size: Average about 3 cm across
Where to look: Lower shores; under rocks and overhangs behind weed
Range: Most European coasts

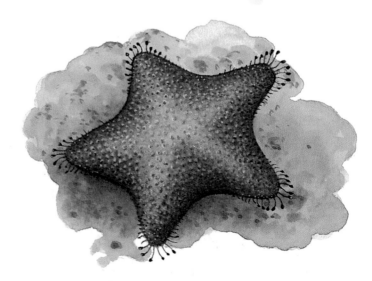

Asterina gibbosa

Feather Star

Feather Stars get their name from their ten feathery arms. These are spread upwards to catch passing fragments of food. They are not starfish but are related to them. Feather stars hold on to rocks and seaweeds with a cluster of small finger-like projections called 'cirri'. They can also swim by 'rowing' with their arms. If you handle one, it will probably break because they are very delicate.

Size: Arms up to 15 cm long
Where to look: Lower rocky shore attached to rocks or seaweed
Range: Most European coasts

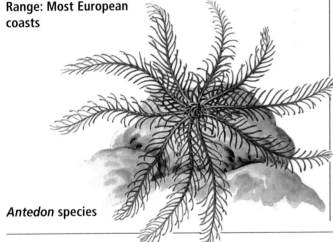

Antedon species

Spiny Brittlestar

Brittlestars have round bodies and much thinner arms than starfish. As their name suggests, you must handle these creatures gently as their arms easily break off. This means they can easily escape if an arm gets trapped under a stone in rough weather. They can then regrow the arm. There are many different species. This one has striped arms with many bristly spines.

Size: Disc up to 2 cm; arms up to 10 cm
Where to look: Lift up stones on lower shores; around seaweed holdfasts
Range: Most European coasts

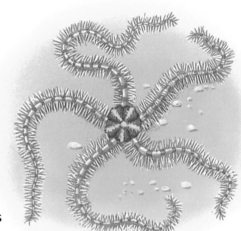

Ophiothrix species

Common Atlantic Octopus

A very secretive and shy mollusc, the Common Atlantic Octopus hides away in caves among rocks. There it waits for a crab to approach. Suddenly it launches itself forward, opens its arms and descends on its prey to seize it with its many suckers. Then the octopus makes a small hole in the shell with its parrot-like beak, injects a fluid and sucks out the crab's body. Each tentacle has two rows of suckers on it. Other similar species have only one.

Size: Up to 1 m or more from tentacle tip to tentacle tip
Where to look: Public aquarium; in holes among rocks at extreme low tide mark
Range: Most European coasts

Octopus vulgaris

Slugs & Shelled Animals

Sea Hare

This is not a true sea slug because it has an internal shell. In most years, in early summer, Sea Hares come inshore in numbers to lay their tangled threads of eggs on rocks and among weed. They feed on sea lettuce and other seaweeds. If you disturb one, you may see it give off a purple liquid which seems to have a defensive effect. Their life lasts a year and they die after spawning.

Size: Average about 10 cm
Where to look: Lower shores, but some years they do not come inshore
Range: Northern coasts; similar species in Mediterranean

Aplysia punctata

Sea Lemon
Archidoris pseudoargus

Although quite common, you will have to search carefully for this sea slug as it is well-camouflaged. They are not always yellow as the name implies. In early summer, it lays whitish, coiled egg ribbons on the underside of rocks. You may find Sea Lemons under rocks where they feed on the breadcrumb sponge. Like all sea slugs, Sea Lemons are hermaphrodites, so every one lays eggs.

Size: Average up to 5 cm, but up to 12 cm maximum
Where to look: Lower shores under rock overhangs among sponges
Range: Northern European shores

Sea Slug

This small sea slug is attractive with its white body and yellow markings. It feeds on Sea Mats and hydroids especially those growing on kelp – a large brown seaweed. You will have to search very carefully because of its size, and although common in some places is less so in others. Note the star-shaped gills at the rear. Look out too for other kinds of sea slugs that live on the shore. Many are brightly coloured.

Size: Up to 4 cm
Where to look: Lower shores on kelp covered in hydroids and Sea Mats
Range: Most European coasts

Polycera quadrilineata

Limpet

Limpets have a 'home' space on the rock. Each time the tide covers them they wander off and browse, and then as the tide ebbs they return to their space. By constantly clamping down they erode a small depression. Look for empty spaces on soft rocks. Feel how strongly limpets can cling on to their rocks.

Size: Up to 6 cm across
Where to look: Rocks on upper and middle shores
Range: Widespread on European coasts

Patella species

Chiton

Search carefully for this creature on rocks, but remember it is small and not too obvious. Also known as the Coat of Mail Shell, it has eight overlapping shell plates, and if you prise one off its rock you will see it curl up. It browses at night and finds its way home by leaving a mucus trail and then returning along it. There are many different kinds of chitons but they are hard to tell apart.

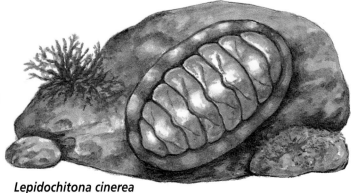

Lepidochitona cinerea

Size: Up to 2 cm, sometimes more
Where to look: Rocky shores, firmly attached to rocks and stones
Range: Most European coasts

Mussel

Mussels are bivalve seashells, that is they have two halves to their shell. They attach themselves firmly on to rocks by secreting fluid threads which quickly harden to form a strong attachment. Mussels feed by filtering particles from seawater. One Mussel may pass as much as a litre of seawater through its body every hour. A Mussel six centimetres long may be seven years old.

Size: Up to 8 cm
Where to look: Very common on rocky shores, often in huge beds in estuaries and sea lochs
Range: Most European coasts

Mytilus **species**

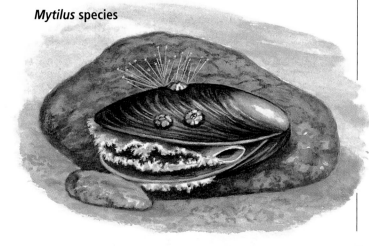

Acorn or Rock Barnacles

Barnacles cover large areas of rock on many shores especially those exposed to waves. Their tough shells can make the rock surface too sharp to walk on without shoes. Look closely at low tide and you will see that the opening in the top is firmly shut to keep moisture in. Those with open holes are dead. When the tide comes in, the doors open up and the barnacle extends its curved, feathery feet to comb the water for food. Barnacles are not sea shells (molluscs), but are crustaceans like crabs and prawns.

Size: Up to 1 cm
Where to look: On the top and middle of rocky shores
Range: Widespread on European coasts

Balanus **species**

Molluscs & Crustaceans

Common Periwinkle

A very common sea snail on all rocky shores, the Periwinkle browses on seaweeds. It is a shell that has adapted to life in a wide variety of habitats from bare rocks to sand, soft mud and estuaries. Periwinkles are often left exposed on a rock by the ebb tide, so they shut their door (operculum) and secrete mucus which sticks them lightly in place. They are commonly called Winkles and are widely eaten.

Size: About 2 cm tall
Where to look: Middle and lower rocky shore and estuaries; look for them making winding trails through smaller muddy pools between rocks
Range: Most European shores

Littorina littorea

Flat Periwinkle

These sea snails have shells with a rich variety of colours, yellow, green, brown, red, black and striped. See how many different colours you can find. If feeding on Bladderwrack, notice how some closely resemble the small bladders. This may help to protect them from seabirds. As the ebb tide exposes them, Flat Periwinkles seek the damp coolness beneath the seaweeds, safe from drying wind and the sun's heat. Their shell is smooth and not pointed like the Common Periwinkle.

Size: About 1 cm across
Where to look: Middle and lower shore among Bladderwrack and Knotted Wrack
Range: Northern European shores

Littorina littoralis

Purple Topshell

Gibbula umbilicalis

Topshells are shaped like small spinning tops. You will often find that this shell has a partly silvery brightness where the outer shell has eroded. Be careful not to confuse it with the Grey Topshell which has finer brownish purple lines. If you keep topshells or periwinkles in your aquarium, they will crawl out of the water and escape, so put some netting over the top.

Size: About 1 cm across
Where to look: Lower rocky shores among seaweeds
Range: Most European shores

Dogwhelk

Dogwhelks are mostly a dirty white, but look out for yellow ones and brown-striped ones. To be sure it is a dogwhelk, look at the shell opening which is oval with a channel cut in one side. It feeds mainly on barnacles and mussels by secreting an acid which softens the shell. It can then bore a hole through the shell with its tough tongue (called a radula). Recently, dogwhelks on many shores stopped laying eggs due to the effect of TBT, an anti-fouling paint used on boats.

Size: About 2 cm
Where to look: Among barnacles and mussels
Range: Northern European shores

Nucella lapillus

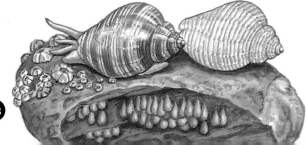

Velvet Swimming Crab

When you turn over a rock and see a reddish-brown, velvety crab with red eyes and its nipper claws snapping at you, it will be a Velvet Swimming Crab. Beware, as it is quick and may give you a painful pinch. Notice its rear pair of legs are flattened and hairy and have bluish lines on them. These enable it to swim and allow it to catch small fish.

Necora puber

Size: Average about 7 cm
Where to look: Under rocks and among seaweed on lower shores
Range: Most European coasts

Edible Crab

You will find the young of this species on the shore. When disturbed, they curl their legs inward and remain motionless. Be careful if you pick one up because it can give you a painful pinch with its powerful, black-tipped claws. Larger specimens live in deeper offshore water. Their reddish colour and oval shell marked like a pie-crust, make them easy to recognize. Their populations are declining due to over-fishing.

Size: Shore average 6 cm; offshore up to 15 cm, occasionally larger
Where to look: Lower shores under rocks
Range: Most European coasts

Cancer pagurus

Green Crab

Also known as the Shore Crab, this is most common crab on almost all rocky shores. You will find some with unequal-sized claws. The smaller one is regrowing after the crab lost the previous one either in a fight or accident. As the crab grows, it moults or casts its old shell. It is then soft for a few days, before hardening once more. Look for cast crab backs on the shore, especially the strandline. In early spring, you may find females carrying masses of orange eggs underneath their bodies. Young Green Crabs less than a centimetre across are often patterned with colours to merge with the sand and rocks. Adults often have two white horse-shoe shapes on their backs.

Size: Up to 4 cm, occasionally larger
Where to look: Almost anywhere on shores
Range: Widespread on European coasts

Carcinus maenas

Crustaceans & Sea Spiders

Marbled Crab

This crab will most likely see you before you see it. Then off it runs at speed and into cover. Marbled Crabs have to avoid the attack of seabirds and their running habit and quick eyesight contribute to their survival. You may find them high on the shore where they survive by keeping their gills moist. They feed on anything they can find lying around. The shell is quite square compared to most other crabs.

Size: Up to 3 cm
Where to look: High up on rocky shores around crevices and shelter
Range: Mediterranean   *Pachygrapsus marmoratus*

Spiny Spider Crab

This crab is also known as the Thornback. As with all crabs, if you find one and need to pick it up, always bring your hand in behind it and grip it across the shell so that it does not pinch you. Sometimes you may be lucky and find one that looks like a walking garden. It has planted seaweeds, sponges and even anemones on its back and spines, all of which provide protection by camouflaging the crab. This crab is fished commercially.

Size: Back up to 15 cm across
Where to look: Lower shores among rocks and seaweed
Range: Most European coasts

Maia squinado

Porcelain Crab

If you turn over a rock and take a close look at its underside, you will probably see some of these crabs. Small and very flattened, they cling tightly to the rock surface. Be careful if you pick one up because this species casts legs very easily. Porcelain Crabs feed by wafting water currents with their hairy mouthparts and filtering particles from the sea.

Size: Up to about 1 cm
Where to look: Under surface of stones on middle and lower shores
Range: Most European coasts

Porcellana species

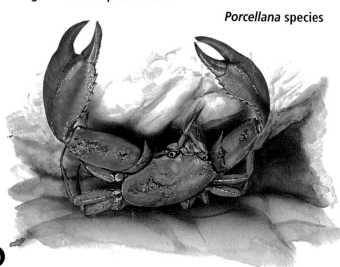

Sponge Crab

This crab has a symbiotic relationship with pieces of sponge. This means that the two live together in a way that benefits both of them. The Sponge Crab carries the sponges on its back, and they grow into its shape, held there by the two pairs of rear legs. These legs, unusual in most crabs, have tiny pincer claws. The sponge appears to offer protection from octopuses, the main predator of sponge crabs. The sponge may benefit by being held up high where it can filter more food from water currents. This is a very slow moving crab which, despite its powerful claws, feeds mainly on plankton.

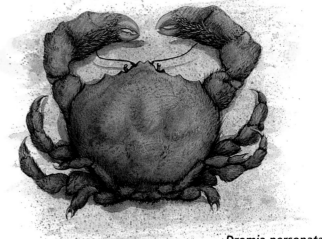

Dromia personata

Size: Up to about 8 cm across
Where to look: Lower rocky shores and in shallows
Range: Southern European coasts north to English Channel

Long-legged Spider Crab

So called because it resembles a spider both in appearance and movement, this crab spends most of its time holding on to rough rock faces or seaweed, with its nipper-claws ready to seize passing small prey. Most small spider crab species 'dress up' by fastening pieces of seaweed on to the spines of their bodies, which is a good method of camouflage.

Size: Body up to 2 cm
Where to look: Rocky shores among weeds; sometimes beneath rocks and ledges
Range: Most European coasts

Macropodia longirostris

Sea Spider (Pycnogonum)

Unrelated to land spiders, these creatures are slow, and have rather chunky bodies and thick legs. They are quite small and not easy to find on columns of sea anemones like the Beadlet or on hydroids where they live. When the female has laid her eggs, the male carries them on his legs.

Size: Up to just over 2 cm
Where to look: On columns of beadlet anemones on lower shores; on hydroids; under stones
Range: Northern European coasts

Pycnogonum species

Sea Spider (Nymphon)

These small delicate animals have legs that look like strands of white cotton. They are slow-moving animals that carefully put each leg in place as they move over hydroids – which they eat – or seaweed. Sea spiders have a fifth pair of legs which are used by the male for holding eggs laid by his mate in the breeding season. They are hard to find, due to their size.

Size: Body 1 cm; legs to 3 cm
Where to look: Collect seafirs and small seaweeds and carefully search through them
Range: Most European coasts

Nymphon gracile

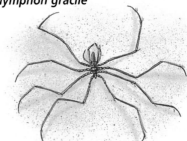

Crustaceans

Common Prawn

This is a beautiful animal to examine with your hand lens. Take a close look at its eyes, its jointed, clawed legs, its mouthparts and its internal organs. To tell a prawn from a shrimp (see below right), look for a long pointed spine (the rostrum) sticking forward between the eyes. A shrimp does not have this and its body is flatter. You may find some prawns with egg clusters on the belly. A small swelling on the side of the head of some specimens is a parasite called an Isopod (see page 46). This crustacean is ideal for your aquarium.

Size: Up to 10 cm
Where to look: Rock pools especially in summer, among seaweed and under ledges
Range: Most European coasts

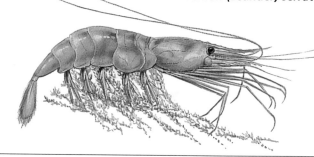

Palaemon (Leander) serratus

Snapping Prawns

These prawns are able to snap their greatly enlarged pincer claw with such force that it sounds like a loud cracking. This sets up vibrations in the water which stun any prey coming close to it. This very unusual method of catching food also gives it its other name, the Pistol Shrimp. You may hear one before you track it down.

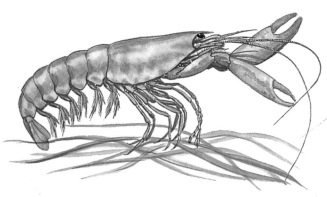

Size: Average up to 3.5 cm
Where to look: Among rocks and weeds on lower shores and in shallow water
Range: Most European coasts

Alpheus species

Opossum Shrimp

Often known as Mysids, these small shrimps are often quite transparent and may suspend themselves in mid-water. If you push your shrimp net through sea grass or over muddy sand in estuaries, you may catch some. If you look closely, you will see females have a brood pouch on their underside. In this the eggs are reared until they are ready to be released as miniature adults.

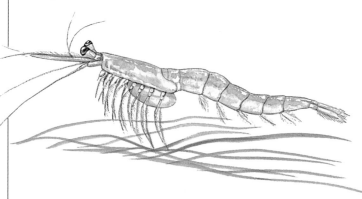

Size: Up to 2 cm
Where to look: Use shrimp net in sea grass or sandy pools
Range: European coasts north of Biscay

Praunus flexuosus

Lobster

Many people think Lobsters are pink because that is the colour they turn when boiled. However, live ones are always blue. Beware of them, as they can crush with one nipper claw and cut with the other. On sandy bottoms among rocks, a lobster will scoop out sand like a bulldozer to make a safe hideaway under a rock. Like other crustaceans, lobsters moult as they grow. They leave behind the whole shell including hairs and the skin over the eyes. These cast shells make good display items.

Size: Average 25 cm; large ones up to 40 cm
Where to look: In summer in rock crevices and holes near low tide mark; public aquariums
Range: Most European coasts

Homarus gammarus

Crawfish

Unlike lobsters, the crawfish has only tiny claws. However, this fascinating crustacean has a shell covered in spines and cutting edges, and two very long, stout antennae. Crawfish feed especially on shellfish which they break open with a pincer-like action of their mouthparts. Unlike lobsters, this species often live together in sheltered rocky places and submarine caves.

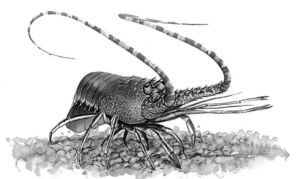

Palinurus elephas

Size: Up to 50 cm
Where to look: Very low on rocky shores and beyond the tidal zone
Range: Most European coasts

Squat Lobster

This is the most brightly coloured crustacean you will find on European shores. When disturbed, it straightens its tail and then suddenly bends it back under its belly. This causes it to jet backwards. Beware if you try to pick one up. It will threaten with its big claws and nip you painfully. This species is not suitable for an aquarium because they tend to hide away. There are several other less colourful species found on the shore.

Size: Up to 12 cm
Where to look:
Deep low tide pools; common in some places, almost absent in others
Range: Most European coasts

Galathea strigosa

Pool Goggling

When the tide goes out, most shore animals hide in crevices, and under rocks and seaweed and wait for the tide to come in again. Rock pools are different. Here the animals can live happily and can carry on feeding and moving about.

You can watch them with a pool goggler. This can be a diver's face mask, a clear plastic dish or you can make a special pool goggler like the one below. Gogglers work best on bright sunny days in well-lit pools; they cut out surface reflections so you can see more clearly into the water.

Make a pool goggler

1 **Find a plastic container** such as an old bucket or wastepaper basket. Get an adult to cut the bottom out leaving a rim about 2–3 cm wide.
2 **Get an adult to cut a piece of perspex** to fit inside the container or buy a piece from a glass shop.

3 **Stick it down on to the rim** with waterproof adhesive – you can buy this from an aquarium stockist. You can use clear plastic instead of perspex, but this is not as strong.

Sea snails

Search in rock pools and among seaweeds for different kinds of sea snails. Put them in a clear plastic jar with some sea water and watch them move about.

As they climb the sides of the jar, you will be able to see the strong foot on which they move. A pair of tentacles will emerge from the front of the animal, with two small black eyes at their bases. Look out for differences between the tentacles and shells of the various species.

Using your goggler

1 **Choose an interesting rock pool.** Sit down at the edge and quietly watch to see who might be at home. If you move suddenly you will frighten fish and other animals and they will hide away.
2 **Gently lower your goggler into the water.** It is safest to lie down on the rocks, so you may need waterproofs or a plastic bin bag.
3 **Watch out for barnacles feeding**, scooping the water with their feathery legs. You may see limpets and sea snails crawling along. Look for shrimps, fish, hermit crabs and sea slugs as well.
4 **Even if you can't see the animals**, look out for trails in the sand or mud on the bottom. Follow one and you may find a periwinkle.

Feeding crabs & anemones

Try getting to know some of your pool animals a bit better by feeding them.

1 **Tie a piece of bait** (such as meat) on to a length of cotton. Crabs will grab hold of it and you can gently pull them out for a closer look.

2 **Make a temporary home for a captured crab** in a bowl with sand, stones and sea water. Let it settle down and then give it some food and watch how it eats. Does it really walk sideways?

3 **Look for an open anemone** and gently touch the tentacles with your finger. It will feel sticky. Anemones capture live animals by shooting tiny stinging threads into them – or into your finger! Most anemones are too small to hurt us, but don't touch large ones.

4 **Try dropping small pieces of bait** on to an open anemone. If it likes the food, the anemone will hold on to the food and eventually push it into its mouth in the middle of the tentacles.

5 **Draw the shape of your rock pool in your field notebook.** Mark in rocks and seaweeds. Then mark in where you have found animals with your goggler. Make a note of what the animals are doing.

6 **Use a small net to search for fish** and shrimps among the seaweeds lining your pool. Try not to disturb the pool too much. Remember that fish will die if kept too long in a bucket.

Hoppers & Sponges

Sea Slater

The Sea Slater resembles a large woodlouse. It lives right at the top of the seashore, where it feeds on plant and animal debris at night. By being active at night it avoids being eaten by seabirds. You can find it by lifting up the debris. You may find a female carrying eggs or young in a brood pouch underneath her. You could keep a Sea Slater for a short time in a plastic dish with a lid with seaweed and a few stones for it to hide under – if you can catch one!

Size: Up to 2.5 cm long
Where to look: Above highwater mark on harbour walls and rocks
Range: Widespread on European shores

Ligia oceanica

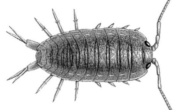

Isopods

Sea slaters and woodlice belong to a group of crustaceans called isopods – a name meaning that the legs are all more or less alike. Many other isopods feed on scraps of plant and animal matter on the lower shore. Unlike the Sea Slater, most of them are good swimmers and they are happy to be submerged at high tide. Most of them are green or brown and well camouflaged.

Size: Up to nearly 2.5 cm long
Where to look: Lower shores among sea grass and seaweeds
Range: Widespread on European coasts

Idotea **species**

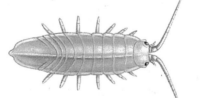

Sandhoppers

If you lift some seaweed on the strandline you will see dozens of these creatures leaping high in the air or burrowing out of sight. They are nocturnal animals and feed on seaweed and animal matter. In the summer, scrape up some sand beneath stranded seaweed and you will find some females with young ones clinging to the brood pouch and others with eggs. If you can keep one still enough, notice how its body is flattened from side to side. They are eaten by turnstones, oystercatchers and fish.

Size: Up to 2 cm
Where to look: Strandline beneath seaweed and in small burrows
Range: Widespread on European coasts

Talitrus **and** *Orchestia* **species**

Breadcrumb Sponge

This green or orange sponge spreads over the underside of rock overhangs and ledges. Sponges are primitive animals which live by drawing in water through a mass of pores, extracting food particles, and then ejecting the clean water through large volcano-like holes. The body is stiffened by masses of sharp prickles called 'spicules'. If you gently press part of this sponge you will see water flow out.

Size: Spreading and variable
Where to look: Under rock overhangs; under rocks; around seaweed holdfasts; lower shores
Range: Most European coasts
Halichondria panicea

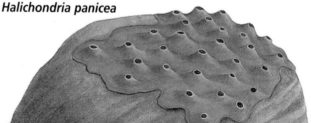

Purse Sponges

These little sponges stand upright like tiny vases. At the top, you will see the large pore through which used water is passed out. This is surrounded by a crown of stiff hairs. You often see a number of these sponges growing together from a single attachment. Look out too for another purse sponge that hangs down from shady damp rocks. Out of water, they look like empty hot water bottles. Despite seeming to be lifeless, sponges are extremely sensitive to habitat conditions.

Size: Up to 3 cm high
Where to look: Lower rocky shores in shady places. Often attached to red seaweeds.
Also on submerged pier supports
Range: Most European coasts

Sycon species

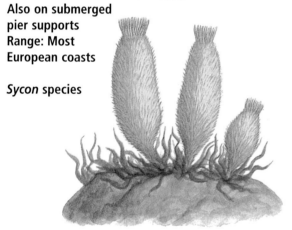

Bath Sponge

This is the large, soft bath sponge you may see in chemist shops. Bath Sponges are collected from deep water in the Greek islands. The part you buy is the 'skeleton', which is made of a soft material called 'spongin'. Most other sponges have sharp 'spicules' in their skeleton and would be no use for washing with. All sponges lack muscles, nerves and sense organs and live by filtering sea water. They are the simplest of the many-celled animals.

Size: Up to 30 cm average
Where to look: On rocks from just below tide level downwards. Most of those in shallow water have been collected
Range: Mediterranean

Spongia officinalis

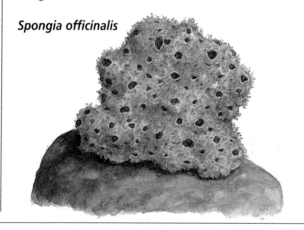

Organ-pipe Sponge

This sponge is shaped as a mass of tiny soft tubes which sprawl over rocks. Small groups of upright tubes grow up from this base, hence the name. However, they really look more like bunches of tiny bananas. Most sponges are difficult to identify, but with careful observation you should soon begin to recognize the common ones shown in this book.

Size: Up to about 3 cm tall   *Leucosolenia botryoides*
Where to look: On rocks and seaweeds on lower shores
Range: Widespread on European coasts

47

Worms

Green Leaf Worm

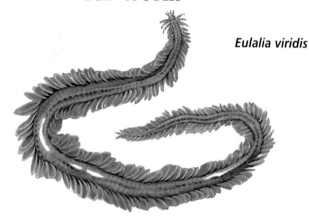

Eulalia viridis

As the tide ebbs, look under the sea wracks growing on rocky platforms and you will soon find this very common but beautiful worm. It feeds mainly on plant and animal debris. Pick up one of these worms carefully and watch it move in a plastic container of seawater. If you are lucky you will see it swim using large leaf-like false legs (parapodia). In summer, you will probably find small pea-sized blobs of soft transparent jelly which contain this worm's green eggs.

Size: Up to 15 cm long
Where to look: On rock surfaces beneath seaweed; especially common among barnacles
Range: Most European coasts

Scale Worm

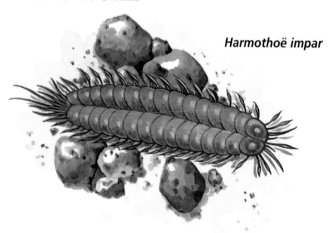

Harmothoë impar

The body of these unusual worms is covered with fifteen pairs of overlapping scales. Other sorts of scale worm have different numbers of scales. They almost glide along, keeping in close contact with a rock surface. They are variable in colour from grey to brown, and some have yellowish markings. Be very careful if you handle one because it may suddenly break into several pieces. It is best to look and not touch.

Size: Up to 2.5 cm
Where to look: Middle and lower shore beneath rocks, often among seaweed
Range: Most European coasts

Worms (Marphysa)

These large and beautiful worms live in narrow rock crevices and so are not too easy to find. They are often iridescent and quite fragile, although they can inflict a painful bite. Look for red, feathery and comb-like gills along the body.

Size: Up to 60 cm long
Where to look: Rock crevices, under stones and on muddy lower shores
Range: Most European coasts

Marphysa species

Keel Worm

You will find Keel Worms all over stones and shells. They look like small tubes opening out wider at one end because, as the worm grows, it needs an ever wider tube in which to live. They are called keel worms because their tubes have a triangular shaped opening and a ridge along the top. Put a stone with some of these creatures on it into a dish of water. Wait a while and with your hand lens you will see the worm extend its crown of red and white tentacles.

Size: Mostly about 2.5 cm long
Where to look: On stones, shells or rocks on lower shores
Range: Widespread around European coasts

Pomatoceros triqueter

Honeycomb Worm

Sabellaria alveolata

If you are exploring a beach with both rocks and sand, and you see a large 'spotty' heap of sand on the side of a rock, look closely. It may be the honeycomb tubes of this worm, which it makes by sticking sand grains together. When covered by the sea, the worm extends its head and feeds on drifting particles.

Size: Makes large sand grain reefs. Individual tubes up to 5 cm
Where to look: Shores with rocks and sand interspersed
Range: Most European shores

Spiral Tube Worms

These worms are easy to spot. You will see their tiny, circular, coiled tubes on brown seaweeds (wracks), shells and stones, often in large numbers. But look closely with your hand lens and you will see that some coil clockwise and others anti-clockwise. They are two different species. Break off a piece of seaweed with a Spiral Tube Worm on it and put it in a dish of water. With a little patience you will see the worm extend its tentacles.

Size: Up to 0.4 mm diameter
Where to look: On brown seaweeds, rocks and shells
Range: Most European shores

Spirorbis species

Plant-like Animals

Sea Fan

This is a pretty little sea fan that branches out in a single plane. It is a horny coral with a 'skeleton' of hard dark material. Along its branches are many tiny anemone-like polyps armed with tentacles to catch plankton. If disturbed, the tentacles quickly retract. Unfortunately it tends to be over-collected by divers and broken by fishing trawls.

Size: Varies up to a spread of 30 cm
Where to look: Mostly seen by divers but look out for sea fans when snorkelling in the Mediterranean
Range: Southern and Western European coasts

Eunicella verrucosa

Stalked Jellyfishes

This is a member of a family of jellyfish that have an adhesive stalk with which they attach themselves to seaweeds and sea grass. The edge of the body is split into eight sections, each with a cluster of tentacles. If food becomes scarce, this jellyfish drifts off to a new area. Search very carefully because they are not easy to find.

Size: Up to 6 cm tall
Where to look: On sea grass, kelps and red seaweeds on lower shores and in pools
Range: Northern European coasts (not Mediterranean)

Haliclystus species

Dead Man's Fingers

So called because when washed up on shore, these soft corals look like swollen, white fingers. They can also be orange. Their mass of spongy material supports large numbers of polyps all united by common food channels. Each polyp has eight feathery tentacles which trap plankton. You may find quite small ones in rock pools. If you touch one, you will see its tentacles immediately withdraw.

Size: Groups up to 25 cm tall and spreading
Where to look: In deep rock pools; on pier piles; strandlines after storms
Range: European coasts north of Portugal

Alcyonium digitatum

Golden Cup Coral

This anemone-like animal lives in its secreted limy skeleton, as does the Devonshire Cup Coral. You may chance upon a group of them which have grown together or sometimes find a solitary one. It shuns daylight so you should search for it in well shadowed places. It is well worth discovering as it is one of the very few European corals.

Size: Up to 1 cm
Where to look: Extreme lower shores in shaded places
Range: Southern European coasts, north to southwest Britain

Leptosammia pruvoti

Devonshire Cup Coral

This is true coral, that is it has a hard stony skeleton. It does not form coral reefs but lives a solitary life from extreme low water and down into deeper sea. The skeleton is shaped like a small cup and the polyp has about fifty tentacles. When you first see one fully expanded, you may think it is an anemone. You can gently feel to see if it has a skeleton. When searching, you may also find some of the limy cups left by dead polyps.

Size: 1 cm tall and up to 2.5 cm across
Where to look: Very extreme low tide on rocks in pools; pier piles or harbour walls; not easy to find so search carefully
Range: Most European coasts

Caryophyllia smithii

Plant-like Animals

Sea Mat

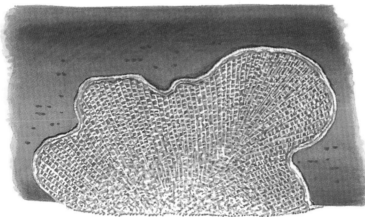

On a low spring tide, search carefully among kelps – large brown seaweeds (see page 28). On their fronds, you will find gauze-like, lacy mats spreading over several centimetres. Your hand lens will reveal a honeycomb mass of oblong cells. Each cell is built by a tiny animal with a fringe of tentacles. These colonies belong to a group of animals called bryozoans, or moss animals. After a storm, look for Sea Mats on stranded seaweeds.

Size: Flattened but spreading over several centimetres
Where to look: On kelp seaweeds; also on stranded seaweed
Range: Widespread on European coasts

Membranipora membranacea

Spiral-tufted Bryozoans

Unlike the flattened Sea Mat, this bryozoan or sea moss colony grows as small tufts resembling miniature Christmas trees. Each small branch of the colony is made up of tiny compartments each housing a tentacled feeding head. Some are shaped like a bird's head and are used to defend and clean the colony but you will need a microscope to see this.

Size: Up to 5 cm
Where to look: Lower shores under overhangs and among seaweeds
Range: Most European coasts

Bugula species

Wineglass Hydroid

You will find these when you are exploring the kelp jungles. Their little zig-zag stems rise in hundreds from the seaweed fronds. Here is a whole new world for you to discover with the aid of your hand lens. You will see their delicate glass-like cups with their rows of transparent tentacles. Look too at those urn-shaped reproductive polyps ready to shed jellyfish-like young that will swim away to found new colonies.

Size: Up to 4 cm high
Where to look: On kelps and other seaweeds, mid and lower shores
Range: Widespread on European shores

Obelia geniculata

Oaten Pipes Hydroid

Colonies of this beautiful hydroid grow on rocks. Upright stems rise up from a mat of creeping 'roots'. Use your lens to see the polyps with two rings of drooping tentacles at the top of each stem. You may be lucky enough to find a polyp with its reproductive bodies looking like a tiny bunch of grapes. The hydroids are all miniature relatives of the sea anemones.

Size: Up to 10 cm or more
Where to look: Rock pools on lower shores; strong current areas, ship wrecks
Range: Most European coasts; related species Mediterranean

Tubularia **species**

Club Hydroid

The more you explore the mysteries of the seashore, the more fascinating small animals you will find. If you look carefully at the masses of brown wrack seaweeds on a rocky shore, you may see small pink bundles attached to them. Your hand lens will reveal a colony of tiny stalks each with a club-shaped head of tentacles. Look for clusters of reproductive buds amongst the tentacles.

Size: 1 to 2 cm
Where to look:
On brown wrack
seaweeds
Range: Northern
European shores

Clava **species**

Feather Hydroid

This small hydroid or sea fir, grows as delicate, feather-shaped colonies. The 'feathers' arise from a mass of thread-like stems that twine around rocks and seaweeds and hold the colony firmly in place. With your hand lens, you should be able to see the tiny feeding heads or polyps arranged along each branch. Look too for yellowish, vase-shaped reproductive bodies.

Size: About 8 cm
Where to look: On rocks and especially on sea oak seaweed in rock pools
Range: Most European coasts

Aglaeophenia **species**

Plant-like Animals

Beadlet Anemone

Actinia equina

The commonest anemone on European shores. When the tide is out, they look like blobs of red, green or brown jelly. Try feeding an open one in a rock pool, with small pieces of shellfish. The tentacles will curl in and slowly push the food into the mouth. If you gently touch the tentacles, they feel sticky. It may shoot out tiny barbed threads to try to sting you. If two anemones touch, one often attacks the other. One of them leans over and stings the other with extra powerful stings held in a ring of blue spots just below the tentacles. The victim crawls away or drops off the rock.

Size: Up to 7 cm
Where to look: On rocky shores from high to low tide
Range: Widespread on most European shores

Anemonia viridis

Dahlia Anemone

You should search for one of these anemones down near the limit of a low spring tide. They keep away from the light and usually wait until after dark to spread their thick tentacles wide. It is then they look like the dahlia flower that they are named after. The Dahlia Anemone attaches many small stones and shell fragments to its body and when its tentacles are withdrawn it is not always easy to find.

Size: Up to 9 cm
Where to look: Lower shores behind seaweed curtains, under rocks and rock overhangs
Range: Northern European coasts

Urticina (Tealia) felina

Snakelocks Anemone

You should find this anemone easy to recognize. Its long green or brown tentacles have violet tips and do not contract when you touch them. It usually grows in pools and places exposed to sunlight. It prefers the light because its tentacles contain microscopic plants which need sunlight to grow. These cells and the anemone have a 'symbiotic relationship' which means that they live together in a way that benefits both of them. The plant cells are protected inside the anemone and in turn provide a clean up service using up the anemone's waste products. This anemone catches small fish and crabs, and so, although easy keep in aquariums, it is not recommended.

Size: Up to 12 cm across
Where to look: Shores in standing water on open, well-lit rocks and in rock pools
Range: European shores, north to Scotland

Gem Anemone

This species often has its column hidden in the crack of a rock, usually covered by water. This column has many sticky areas which hold sand and shell fragments. These may be for protection against wave action or the sun's heat. When searching, look closely because the disc of tentacles is usually spread against the rock surface. When exposed by the tide, the tentacles are retracted.

Size: Up to 6 cm across tentacles
Where to look: Rock pools especially among coral weed (*Corallina*). Also on rocks next to sand
Range: European coasts north to Britain

Bunodactis verrucosa

Plumose Anemone

Also known as the Frilled Anemone, this is a plankton-feeding anemone. It has very many fine tentacles, each with many fine 'hairs'. These wave to and fro, and waft plankton towards the mouth. They are far too delicate to cope with the larger prey eaten by other anemones. When feeding, the Plumose inflates with seawater and its column grows very long. When at rest, it is a mere button-like lump. It is usually white or orange, but may be brown, grey or greenish.

Size: 15 cm or more when feeding; 2 cm at rest
Where to look: Pier piles, jetties and harbour walls; small individuals among low-tide seaweeds
Range: European coasts from France northwards

Metridium senile

Jewel Anemone

The tentacle tips of this beautiful little anemone end in tiny round knobs. They are called jewel anemones because they occur in brilliant colours: green, red, orange, pink and white – they seem to sparkle like jewels. They reproduce by dividing in half and so you will usually find them in large groups. Many biologists think they are closely related to corals.

Size: Can be 2.5 cm across when open
Where to look: Lower shores under rock overhangs
Range: Most European coasts north at least to Scotland

Corynactis viridis

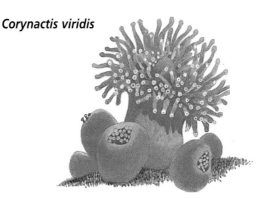

Animals Living Together

Parasitic Anemone

Despite its name, this sea anemone is not a parasite. It grows on old whelk shells inhabited by hermit crabs and helps the crab by providing all those stinging tentacles to repel hungry fish and octopuses. Some hermits have two or more anemones on their whelk-shell homes. In return, the anemone gets taken to fresh feeding grounds, and it also gets some of the hermit crab's left-overs. Hermit crabs are messy feeders and the anemone can bendover and pick up fallen scraps of food.

Size: Up to 8 cm tall
Where to look: On hermit crabs living in large shells; very low on the shore; strandlines after storms
Range: European coasts, north to English Channel

Calliactis parasitica

Fish Louse

These are a kind of copepod (see page 14) that live out their lives clinging to and crawling about on the bodies of fish. The best known is *Argulus* which has two suckers on its underside. You may see species of fish lice clinging on the bodies of a fish you have caught. Others may be firmly attached to gills or even inside the fish's mouth. They suck the fish's blood.

Size: 10–25 mm, according to species
Where to look: Sometimes on fish in aquariums; on recently caught fish
Range: Throughout European waters

Various species

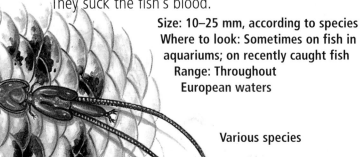

Snail Fur

To find a colony of these hydroids, you will first have to find a hermit crab. Look carefully at the shell to see if it is covered in a soft, pink down, especially around the shell opening. If you examine it with a hand lens, you will see a pink covering from which rise tiny white stalks with a ring of tentacles at the top. These are the feeding polyps. Other pink stalks, with oval sacs, are reproductive individuals.

Size: About 1 cm high
Where to look: On hermit crab shells; rarely on stones
Range: Most European coasts

Cloak Anemone

The pink spotted base of this anemone actually surrounds most of the shell in which the hermit crab lives and the tentacles hang down underneath. If disturbed, the anemone shoots out sticky, clinging threads. To save the hermit looking for a larger shell as it grows, the Cloak Anemone secretes a horny substance which gives more 'living room'. This relationship helps the anemone because the crab takes it to fresh feeding areas. In return, the crab is protected by the stinging tentacles.

Size: About 5 cm across tentacles
Where to look: Sandy or muddy shores in the shallows; not very common
Range: Most European coasts

Adamsia palliata

Horse Mackerel

Up to about one year old, small groups of horse mackerel may be seen swimming in the shelter of jellyfish 'umbrellas'. As they grow larger, they form shoals and spend time around wrecks and reefs. Anglers frequently catch them when mackerel fishing. They lay their eggs in early summer and these change into larvae that drift in the plankton.

Size: Up to 45 cm
Where to look: Public aquariums; anglers' catches; with large jellyfish
Range: Most European waters

Trachurus **species**

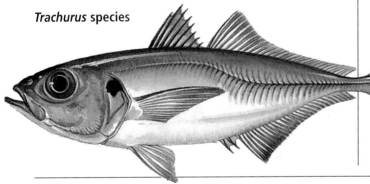

Pearlfish

Carapus acus

Here is a most remarkable relationship. The Pearlfish actually lives within the body cavity of a sea cucumber, often with one or two others. It enters through the cucumber's rear end. Sometimes the sea cucumber pushes the Pearlfish out, together with its own intestines and then quickly grows a new intestine. Do not try to keep sea cucumbers in the aquarium as some species may poison your fish.

Size: Up to 20 cm
Where to look: Search among sea cucumbers on lower shores; public aquariums
Range: Mediterranean

Pea Crab

When you open some mussels or cockles, you may find this small crab inside. It will be a female who lives there feeding on some of the food the mussel draws in. She herself is drawn into the shell as a tiny crab and will grow large and stay there. The male is free living.

Size: Up to 1.5 cm
Where to look: Inside mussels or cockles
Range: Most European coasts

Pinnotheres pisum

Is This Beach Empty?

Flat, sandy beaches may look rather boring at first sight. There are no seaweed-covered rocks and no rock pools full of shrimps, crabs, fish and colourful anemones. However, a great many animals do live here, but when the tide goes out, they have to beat a hasty retreat away from the sun, wind and hungry predators.

Some follow the receding tide down the beach, while others hide under the surface of the sand.

To see these animals, you will have to dig. But before you start, take a walk at low tide along the sea's edge and search in the wet, squidgy sand. Many animals feed at the water's edge and follow the tide as it goes down. You may find slow-moving necklace shells and two-shelled molluscs. They are all well disguised, so search carefully.

Sand search

Sand animals are fussy about the sort of sand they live in. Large, coarse sand allows water to drain away quickly and it soon becomes too dry. Most sand animals prefer fine sand with some mud in it.

1 **Choose a beach which has some mud** in it or squelch your way on to a sticky mud flat.
2 **Look for clues to tell you where to dig** – many worms have tubes that stick up out of the sand. **Be careful:** the mud can be very deep.
3 **Lugworms live in U-shaped burrows** and send up a squiggly cast (pile) of unwanted sand at one end. There is a shallow depression at the head end of the burrow.
4 **Wading birds love eating a juicy worm** or clam and know just where to find them. So try digging where there are flocks of oystercatchers, or other shore birds.
5 **Razor shells send up squirts of water** as you walk over the top of them. They are very fast diggers and you would be lucky to catch one!

Digging up sand dwellers

1 **Dig down with a trowel** as deep as possible.
2 **Put the sand into a large kitchen sieve** and dip it into a pool or a bucket of water.

3 **Shake it gently** so that the sand is washed away leaving you with a collection of worms, clams, heart urchins and sand hoppers. Put your catch into a bucket of sea water.

4 **Try digging at different shore levels.** You will probably find more animals lower down.
5 **Keep a record** of what sort of, and how many, animals you find. Then you can compare different beaches.
6 **When you have finished looking at your catch**, it is important to put the animals back where you found them. Dig shallow holes, put one in each and watch them burrow down, or cover them up.

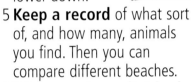

What has the tide left?

At each high tide the sea leaves behind a straggling collection of seaweed, dead animals, shells, driftwood, plastic bottles and other rubbish. It looks a nasty, smelly mess! However, by searching carefully, you will find many treasures. One of the best times to search is after a storm.

Be careful when searching! There may be lumps of oil and tar, or sharp objects. Leave canisters and other unknown containers alone, in case they contain harmful chemicals. Look out for:
1 **Floating animals that have got stranded:** Look at pages 14–17 to help decide what they are. Don't touch jellyfish as they may still sting. Among the seaweed, you may find masses of the hornwrack, a plant-like moss animal that sometimes gets torn from the rocks by storms.
2 **Tough egg cases of fish and molluscs:** The mermaid's purses of skates and rays have horn-like corners; dogfish and small shark cases have long curly tendrils. Whelks lay their eggs in sponge-like masses. Pretty curled collars made of sand grains are the egg strings of necklace shells.
3 **Mollusc shells, sea and heart urchin shells** (called tests), and empty crab shells.
4 **Rotting seaweed.** If you lift it up, the sand will usually erupt as hundreds of sand hoppers jump erratically about.

Sandy Shores & Shallows

Sandy beaches are wonderful places for a holiday. They are ideal for swimming, sand castles and games. But under the sun umbrellas and beach towels, you will find not only people, but also a wealth of living seashells, worms, sandhoppers and other creatures. There are no rocks for the animals to cling on to or hide under. So most of them live buried beneath the sand.

Some sandy beaches are better than others for searching for animals. Coarse sand, gravel and pebbles do not make good homes. The water drains away quickly when the tide goes out and there is very little food available. So muddy sand is better for the animals. Lugworms and heart urchins actually eat sand and digest all the bits of plant and animal material in it. Worm casts are the undigested, sandy remains.

In general, more animals live near the water's edge where the sand is only exposed to the air for a short time. Small pools, odd rocks, old shells and pebbles provide hiding places for shrimps and young flatfish.

High up on the shore, the strandline is also a good hunting place. Here piles of rotting seaweed and other rubbish provide a home for sandhoppers, beach flies and small crabs. This picture shows eleven animals from this book; see how many you can identify.

Burrowing Anemone, Brittlestar, Cockle, Little Cuttle, Lugworm, Ragworm, Sandmason, Sea Potato, Sand Starfish, Tellin, Lesser Weverfish.

Seahorse

The Seahorse uses its tail to grip on to sea grass and catches small crustaceans by suddenly sucking in water and prey. The female Seahorse lays her eggs in a pouch on the male's belly. He carries them until they hatch and then releases them as tiny pin-sized baby Seahorses. Many species are now protected because of over-collecting.

Size: Up to 15 cm
Where to look: Use net in sea grass beds. Snorkel in shallow water
Range: Mediterranean north to Brittany; a few rare migrants in English Channel

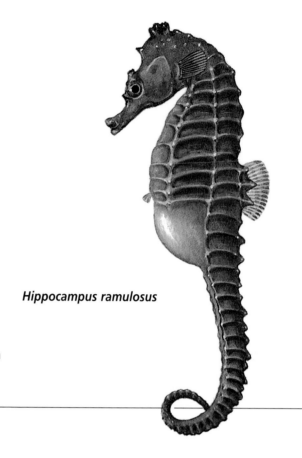

Hippocampus ramulosus

Pipefish

You should look for these creatures in the summer months when they come into the shore. They feed on small crustaceans. The Pipefish's mouth opening is tiny, so it watches its prey closely and then suddenly sucks in a jet of water together with the prey. The male has a brood pouch on its belly and carries the young until they are ready to swim.

Size: Up to 47 cm
Where to look: Use net among seagrass and in rock pools among seaweed
Range: Most European coasts

Syngnathus species

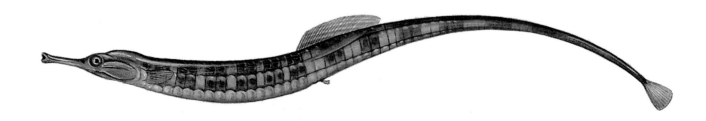

Sand Goby

This sand-coloured, little fish is well camouflaged. If you watch very shallow pools with a sandy bottom you may well see one dart a short distance, stop and merge into the background. In some places they are quite common and easily seen. This species sometimes forms small shoals of as many as thirty. They often lay their eggs in small shells.

Size: Average about 6 cm
Where to look: Shallow sandy pools on shore and estuaries. At the end of summer, you may find pools with thousands of tiny young
Range: Most European coasts

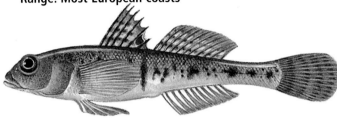

Pomatoschistus minutus

Pogge

Also called the Hooknose, this attractive small fish may be found in spring among the seaweeds growing from harbour and pier walls below low tide level. Here it lays eggs among the holdfasts and these take as long as ten months to hatch. The barbels on the underside of its jaws help it to detect the small crabs, prawns and shrimps on which it feeds.

Size: Average about 10–15 cm
Where to look: Push net through mud, sand or stones in shallows
Range: Northern European waters

Agonus cataphractus

Sand Eels

These fish swim together in shoals often numbering thousands of individuals. When attacked by fish such as mackerel, the Sand Eel escapes by diving headfirst into the sand. It is able to 'swim' a short distance through the sand. Occasionally, large numbers can be seen at the sea's edge during low spring tides, and in summer they are often driven inshore by schools of mackerel.

Size: Up to 30 cm; average about 12 cm
Where to look: Watch shoals swimming past piers and jetties. Wade in deep sandy pools and shuffle up the sand
Range: Most European coasts; a similar species in Mediterranean

Ammodytes species

Fish

Plaice

The orange spots on the topside should allow you to tell plaice from other flatfish. All flatfish start life swimming upright like other fish. Then, they slowly settle on to either their left or right side. The eye on the underside moves to the upper side. Plaice is a favourite edible species. A large female may lay as many as half a million eggs but comparatively few survive to adults because they are eaten by other fish, by seals and by humans!

Size: Offshore up to 90 cm; much smaller in shallow water
Where to look: Small ones in pools on sheltered sandy beaches; public aquariums
Range: Throughout European waters

Pleuronectes platessa

Angler Fish

Lophius piscatorius

This fish is well named, as it fishes for other fish. Its body is surrounded by small flaps of skin which help to camouflage it. Its mouth is enormous and armed with large, backward-pointing, sharp teeth. It lies very still and waits for a small fish to come near. Then it begins to wave its lure which is a long spine with a small flap on its end. The prey fish tries to seize the lure, the Angler's moth opens and the prey is swallowed.

Size: Average about 1 m long
Where to look: You will probably only see this fish in public aquariums but it is worth looking for!
Range: Throughout European waters

Gurnard

These fish communicate with each other by loud grunting sounds when they are swimming in shoals. These sounds are produced by using muscles attached to the swim bladder. A few occur in shallow water but most are found at depths of thirty metres or more. Their main food is crabs, shellfish and fish. Gurnards use the finger-like spines of their pectoral fins to feel over the sand surface for this food.

Size: Average about 60 cm
Where to look: Usually only seen by snorkellers and divers. A favourite public aquarium fish
Range: Throughout European waters

Trigla lucerna

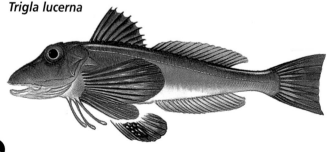

Thornback Ray

This fish is called a Thornback because its back and tail are well covered with stiff prickles. It is also called a Roker. It attaches its egg capsules to seaweed. A single female may lay as many as fifteen each year. You may have seen an empty one washed ashore by storms. It is known as a Mermaid's Purse and is dark with a long horn at each corner. (Dogfish mermaid's purses have long tendrils at each corner.) This fish is a predator on other small fish and crabs.

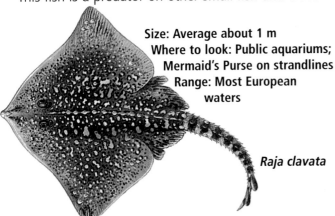

Size: Average about 1 m
Where to look: Public aquariums;
Mermaid's Purse on strandlines
Range: Most European
waters

Raja clavata

Weever Fish

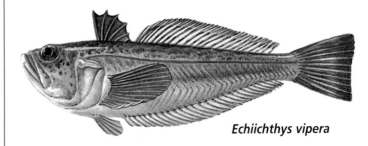

Echiichthys vipera

Beware of this fish! When exploring a sandy beach it is a good idea to wear some sort of footwear because Weever Fish burrow into the sand and have a dorsal fin sticking up. This fin is armed with poison spines, and if you step on it, it can be very painful. (For treatment, see page 18.) The Weever Fish feeds on shrimps and sand eels and tends to move up the shore with a rising tide and down again on the ebb.

Size: Average about 10 cm
Where to look: Be careful when using shrimp net on sand
Range: Most European waters

Stingray

Do not touch this fish! Stingrays are one of the most dangerous fish in European waters. This ray has a long, sharp spine on its tail which can injure you and inject a poison. The sting is very painful. For treatment, see page 18. The Stingray produces quite large, living young.

Size: Up to 1.5 m
Where to look: Calm, shallow water. Take care when wading in sand and mud in warm waters; public aquariums
Range: European waters, not common north of English Channel

Dasyatis pastinaca

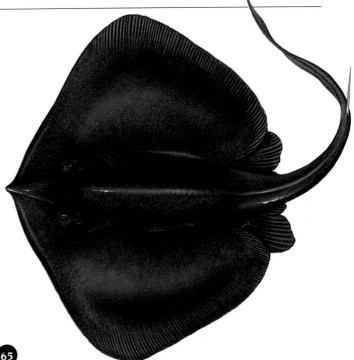

Echinoderms

Sea Potato

If you explore some sandy beaches at low spring tide you may find many of these urchins, also known as Heart Urchins. They burrow some ten centimetres down, but keep contact with the surface with special, extra-long tube feet. These often leave a star-shaped depression in the sand. That is the place for you to dig. If you examine one with your hand lens, you will see the paddle-shaped digging spines. Put the urchin back on the sand and watch it bury itself again.

Size: Up to 9 cm long
Where to look: Sheltered sandy shores near low tide; empty shells on strandlines
Range: Most European coasts

Echinocardium cordatum

Seven-armed Starfish

This starfish uses its feet to push sand aside so that it sinks downwards. It hunts sea urchins, other starfish and sea cucumbers for food. However, the black sea urchin (see page 33) defends itself by flattening its spines and gripping the starfish's skin with tiny, venomous nipper spines. The starfish at once retreats. This species easily loses an arm so many specimens will be regenerating one.

Size: Up to 60 cm across
Where to look: Occasionally found on lower shore
Range: Most European coasts

Luidia ciliaris

Sand Brittlestar

This brittlestar moves about by 'rowing' itself across the sand with its arms. Because of the snake-like movements of these arms these creatures are also known as Serpent Stars. Some live on the sand surface, and some burrow into sand, perhaps to protect their fragile bodies. They extend one or two arms up to the surface to collect food fragments.

Size: Disc up to 3 cm
Where to look: Strandlines and low on sandy shores
Range: Most European coasts

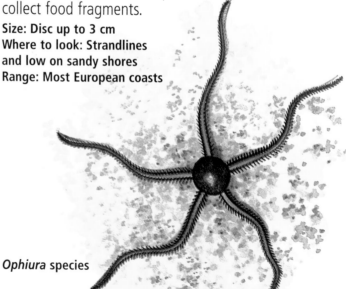

Ophiura species

Purple Heart Urchin

These urchins are not common everywhere, but you may find one on a gravelly or coarse sandy shore at low tide limit. If you look very carefully at the underside with your lens, you may see a tiny bivalve shell (called *Montacuta*) attached to its spines. As with so many seashore creatures, you will find your hand lens reveals wonderful details of the way this sea urchin is made.

Size: Up to 12 cm long
Where to look: Low tide in burrow in gravelly or coarse sand
Range: Most European coasts

Spatangus purpureus

Worm Cucumber

This finger-like sea cucumber has a thin translucent skin and a ring of twelve branched tentacles around its mouth. These are used to select food particles. Its body has a sticky feel because it has minute hooks in it. This will help you to tell it apart from a worm. It lives in a burrow and on its body lives a small bivalve shellfish called *Devonia*.

Size: 20–30 cm long
Where to look: Buried in sand and gravel
Range: Northwards from French coast

Leptosynapta species

Sand Star

This starfish spends much of its life moving through sand, just below the surface. It is easy to recognize. Look for the fringe of spines and bead-like plates around the arms. Its tube feet are pointed and adapted for burrowing, whereas most starfishes' tube feet have sucker discs for gripping. It is a hungry predator on the shellfish, worms and crustaceans it finds under the sand. Prey is swallowed whole and the empty shell or skeleton disgorged a little while later.

Size: Average about 10 cm
Where to look: Sandy shores at low tide; sometimes on the surface; search with torch after dark
Range: Most European coasts

Astropecten irregularis

Molluscs & Crustaceans

Squid

The squid is a fast swimmer, using water-jet propulsion in the same way as the cuttlefish. It attacks shoals of fish, shrimps and crabs, catching them by shooting out two long suckered tentacles which fasten on to the prey's body. Squid chew their prey with a pair of horny jaws that are shaped like an upside down parrot's beak. Their eggs hang in white bunches on seaweed and mooring ropes.

Size: Up to 60 cm long
Where to look: Fishmongers and fish markets; occasionally hooked by anglers; egg mass sometimes on strandlines
Range: Throughout European waters

Loligo forbesii

Little Cuttle

These are wonderful little creatures to keep in your aquarium. Feed them on tiny live shrimps. Little Cuttles shuffle into the sand and use their arms to push sand grains over themselves. When prey comes near, they erupt from the sand and seize it in their suckered tentacles. Their bright eyes see anything moving close by and their bodies constantly change colour.

Size: Up to 5 cm long
Where to look: Use your shrimp net at low tide in the sandy shallows; best catches will be after dark
Range: European waters: very similar species in Mediterranean

Sepiola atlantica

Cuttlefish

With eyes as sensitive as human's, the Cuttlefish hunts shrimps and small fish. It has eight suckered arms and two long tentacles. These can be shot out to grasp prey as much as twenty centimetres away. The Cuttlefish uses its breathing tube as a jet propulsion unit. This enables it to make sudden turns and movements in any direction. It also communicates with other Cuttlefish by rapid colour changes. It lays its black grape-like eggs in sea grass in summer.

Size: Average about 20 cm long
Where to look: Public aquariums; among sea grass; cuttlebone on strandlines; often seen in sandy areas when snorkelling
Range: Most European waters

Sepia officinalis

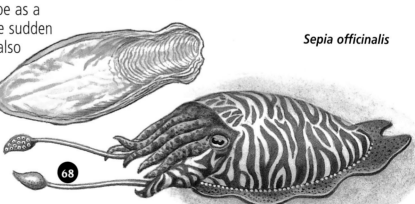

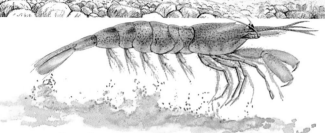

Sand Shrimps

Crangon species

Also called the Brown Shrimp, these animals are very common on most shallow sandy shores and in river estuaries. During daylight, they spend much time half-buried in the sand as a defensive measure against fish. Compare it to the common prawn on page 42. Notice how it is flattened from the top while the pawn is flattened sideways. When you catch one of these creatures, place it in a shallow sandy pool and watch it bury itself. Notice how well camouflaged it is. Sand Shrimps can stand temperatures from freezing up to 30° Centigrade.

Size: Up to 5 cm
Where to look: Use your shrimp net at low tide on sandy shore shallows
Range: Most European coasts

Mantis Shrimps

Some species lurk at the mouth of a burrow waiting for a prey fish to come near. Their eyes can swing and rotate to watch prey better. With lightning speed, the Mantis Shrimp's front legs lash out and can cut a small fish in half. This creature is thought by many scientists to be the most intelligent crustacean.

Size: 12–25 cm
Where to look: In sand and mud and on rocky reefs from extreme low water downwards
Range: Most European coasts

Squilla species

Box Crab

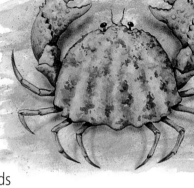

To defend itself against a predator, this crab pulls its legs in tight against its body to form a sort of box. It lives under the sand and extends two small tubes to the surface. These allow water to pass through and so assist breathing. It places itself so that its eyes protrude above the sand's surface to see what is happening around it.

Calappa granulata

Size: Up to 10 cm
Where to look: Rare; sandy and muddy shores
Range: Mediterranean and north to Portugal

Masked Crab

This crab burrows into the sand, leaving its pair of antenna sticking out. These have interlocking hairs that form a tube which prevents sand entering but allows water to flow down for breathing purposes. Mating occurs in early summer after dark; the male grips a female with its long claws, and carries her around. By staying buried in daylight, they avoid predators such as large fish and gulls. Can you see why it is called a Masked Crab?

Size: Body about 4 cm
Where to look: Sheltered sandy shores in early summer especially after dark; strandline after storms
Range: Most European coasts

Corystes cassivelaunus

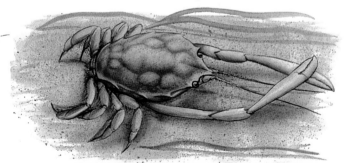

Anemones & Worms

Carpet Anemone

This pretty anemone is wide and flat with many very short, knobbed tentacles that resemble the pile of a carpet. This makes it easy to recognize although its colour is variable. It lives attached to rocks or, more commonly, unattached in sand and mud where its broad base acts as an anchor. If you touch one, it will rapidly pull itself down into the sand.

Size: Up to about 7 cm across
Where to look: Very low on the shore; uncommon
Range: European coasts north to Irish Sea

Aureliana heterocera

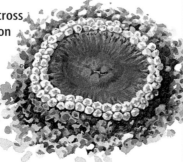

Burrowing Anemone

This anemone is a real burrower. It lives in sand or gravel and digs down as far as 30 centimetres. Unlike the Carpet Anemone, it does not attach to a buried stone. To feed, it extends its twelve long tentacles from the mouth of the burrow. If at all disturbed, it retreats quickly downwards. Its larvae are parasitic on tiny jellyfish. It was named after Charles Peach, a Victorian coastguard and naturalist.

Size: Up to 12 cm across tentacles
Where to look: In sand or gravel very low on the shore; common offshore
Range: European shores

Peachia hastata

Lugworms

Lugworms live in U-shaped burrows on muddy sand and sandy shores. As each one burrows, it takes in mouthfuls of sand from which it takes its food. The waste is then pushed up like toothpaste out of a tube and lies on the surface like a coiled worm. Nearby is the 'blow-hole' where the Lugworm draws down water to breathe.

Size: Up to 25 cm
Where to look: Sandy beaches; estuaries in mud and sand; largest worms mid and lower shores
Range: Most European coasts

Arenicola species

Sea Mouse

If you find one of these creatures, rinse the mud off it and discover its hidden beauty. You will see its body is covered with hair and along its sides are translucent bristles in all colours of the rainbow. It is a type of scale worm but the scales are hidden by the bristles on its back. It crawls through sea-bed deposits feeding on carrion and plant fragments.

Size: Average about 12 cm
Where to look: Strandlines after storms
Range: Most European coasts

Aphrodite aculeata

Ragworms

This family of worms has black, horny jaws used for seizing prey. Large specimens may give you a painful nip so be careful. In muddy estuaries, you may find fifty or more of these worms below a square metre of mud. There they are an important food for many waders. One species lives in a hermit crab's shell. Ragworms are good swimmers.

Size: 10–30 cm
Where to look: Estuary mud;
under rocky shore rocks;
in Hermit Crab's shell
Range: Most European coasts

Nereis **species**

Catworm

Sometimes when you dig for lugworms or turn over sand you will see this pearly-sheened worm wriggling for cover. It is an extremely active worm. It lives in the sand and hunts for prey which it seizes in its powerful jaws. Put one on flat wet sand and watch it burrow into cover. How long did it take?

Size: 8–10 cm
Where to look: Sand
on lower shore
Range: Most
European coasts

Nephtys hombergi

Ice-cream Cone Worms

These worms make very fragile tubes, open at both ends, by cementing grains of sand together. The delicate beauty of these cones is a wonderful example of building. An open end means the cone is empty, but a door of golden hairs tells you the worm is at home. It lives upside down with its head buried in the sand and the thin end of the tube sticking up.

Size: Up to nearly 7 cm
Where to look: Sandy shores,
often found empty
Range: Most European coasts

Pectinaria **species**

Sandmason Worm

This worm lives in a tube made of sand grains and shell debris. The tufted upper ends of the tubes, projecting above the surface like miniature dish mops, are unmistakable. The fat pink to brown body remains in the tube but it extends long sticky tentacles to feed on the debris that collects around the tube. Living up to its name, this worm is an expert builder. It can sort out sand grains into sizes with its sensitive mouth. Smaller grains are selected for the tufts at the end. The grains are stuck together with mucus.

Size: Up to 30 cm
Where to look: On sandy
shores near low tide level
usually in groups
Range: Most European
coasts

Lanice conchilega

Keep Them at Home

Large aquariums with tropical marine fish are expensive and difficult to keep in good condition. For beginners, it is much easier and just as much fun to run a small aquarium using seashore animals you have collected yourself.

Animals living on the shore are used to quite large changes in temperature and in the saltiness of the water, and so are mostly quite tough characters. If you do decide to keep an aquarium remember:
- You will need your parents' permission and help
- You are responsible for the lives of your animals

Setting up

1 **Buy a fish tank** of a convenient size from a pet shop. They are quite cheap.
2 **You will also need to buy an aerator.** Any type will do – it is just a small pump to bubble air through the water and stop it going stale.
3 **Put a thin layer of shelly sand** in the bottom of the tank. You can collect this yourself. You do not need an under-gravel filter provided you do not keep too many animals. Add some stones and rocks.
4 **Fill up the tank with fresh sea water.** You can use artificial sea water, but this will add to the cost. Do not put any brown seaweeds in the tank – they usually die and will spoil the water. Only put small red or green seaweeds in if you have proper lighting (see 6 below).
5 **Put the tank in a permanently shaded spot** in a cool room. The temperature needs to stay below about 18° Centigrade.
6 **You will need to light your tank** to see the animals properly. Ordinary lights will do but as these give out heat, you should only turn them on for a short time. A film of green algae may grow on the tank sides. If you keep winkles, they will graze on this.
7 **Leave the tank for a few days** and then put a good mix of animals in the tank, but not too many! **Don't try** to keep large crabs or starfish as they will eat your other animals.

Maintenance

If your tank is not covered, the water will evaporate and get saltier. So you must top it up with tap water (let it stand overnight in a bowl first to get rid of the chlorine). Every month, siphon out two-thirds of the water and replace it with fresh sea water.

Suitable animals

You can keep all sorts of animals in your aquarium but the ones listed here will do best and need least attention. Do not prise animals off rocks, but find ones attached to small stones that you can collect.

chiton winkles topshell

limpet tubeworm mussels

barnacles whelk sea urchin

anemones starfish Hermit crab

- **Chitons, winkles, whelks, topshells, limpets, tube worms, mussels, barnacles, and small urchins:** These will mostly feed themselves. They scrape algae from the tank sides and rocks or filter particles from the water. They should be released after a couple of months and new ones collected.
- **Small anemones and rock pool fish:** They will need individual feeding with small pieces of raw fish or meat, once or twice a week.
- **Crabs, hermit crabs, shrimps, sand hoppers and starfish:** They will feed themselves from scraps of fish and meat put in the tank.
- **Dogwhelks:** They need barnacles to feed on.

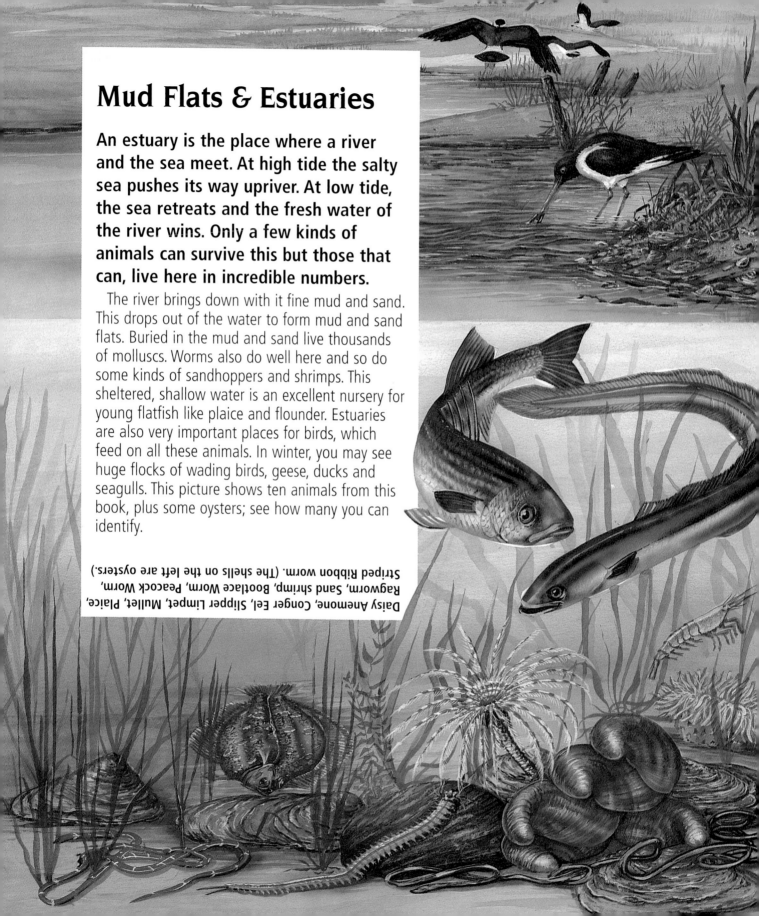

Mud Flats & Estuaries

An estuary is the place where a river and the sea meet. At high tide the salty sea pushes its way upriver. At low tide, the sea retreats and the fresh water of the river wins. Only a few kinds of animals can survive this but those that can, live here in incredible numbers.

The river brings down with it fine mud and sand. This drops out of the water to form mud and sand flats. Buried in the mud and sand live thousands of molluscs. Worms also do well here and so do some kinds of sandhoppers and shrimps. This sheltered, shallow water is an excellent nursery for young flatfish like plaice and flounder. Estuaries are also very important places for birds, which feed on all these animals. In winter, you may see huge flocks of wading birds, geese, ducks and seagulls. This picture shows ten animals from this book, plus some oysters; see how many you can identify.

Daisy Anemone, Conger Eel, Slipper Limpet, Mullet, Plaice, Ragworm, Sand shrimp, Bootlace Worm, Peacock Worm, Striped Ribbon worm. (The shells on the left are oysters.)

Mullet

On warm summer days in quiet estuaries, you may see Mullet basking in the warm surface water. You will see their backs actually breaking the surface. They spawned here in early spring and by early autumn large shoals of babies, four cm long, swim among the seaweeds. Mullet have mouths with large fleshy lips, ideal for browsing on algae.

Size: Up to 60 cm or more
Where to look: Quiet, still estuaries; harbours in late summer
Range: Most European coasts and estuaries

Liza species

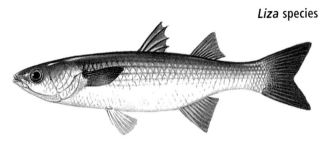

Slipper Limpet

This shell is so-called because when turned over it looks a little like a slipper. Often as many as ten may live one on top of another. The lower ones are females, the middle ones changing sex and the youngest at the top are males. The Slipper Limpet feeds by trapping tiny plants and animals in a mucus 'net'. Every few minutes, the limpet takes the loaded mucus into its mouth and extracts the food particles.

Size: Variable according to position; average 4 cm long
Where to look: Mussel and oyster beds on their shells; strandlines
Range: Spreading around European coasts; an introduced American species

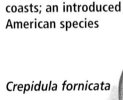

Crepidula fornicata

Bass

Bass form schools and swim into estuaries between May and September. In autumn, they go out to sea and come into shallows around the coast. In gales, they swim in the roughest of surf feeding on shellfish, crabs and lugworms bulldozed out of the sand by the waves. Often they hunt along rock surfaces for prawns. Bass live for a long time, some for over forty years. By law, anglers have to return small ones to the water.

Size: Maximum 1 m; usually about 40 cm
Where to look: Public aquariums; fishmongers
Range: Most European coasts

Dicentrachus labrax

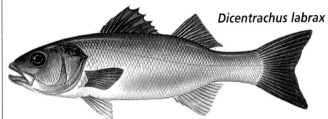

Spire Shell

In muddy estuaries at low tide, the tiny Spire Shell burrows a little way down. You will see thousands of them, like grains of rice. As the tide comes in, the tiny shell comes up and floats shorewards under the surface film. It uses a raft made of mucus to do this and the raft also collects food. On the ebb tide, it is carried back and burrows again. It is an important food for many wading birds. In some areas there may be over 30,000 in every square metre of mud.

Size: Maximum 6 mm
Where to look: On mud in estuaries. In some places, whole beaches may be made up of their dead shells
Range: Most European coasts

Hydrobia ulvae

Daisy Anemone

This beautiful burrowing anemone has up to 700 short, thin tentacles. You may find one living in a crevice in a rock pool. You will see its tentacles spread out on the rock or sand. If you touch it, it immediately retreats into its burrow. If the pool has a muddy bottom, this anemone may push its base down until it contacts a stone or shell and then fastens on to it.

Size: Tentacle disc up to 10 cm or more, usually 3 to 7 cm
Where to look: Rock pools with muddy
or sandy bottom; rock crevices
Range: European coasts
north to Scotland

Cereus pedunculatus

Tube Anemone

This anemone was first named by a Victorian naturalist called Philip Henry Gosse who wrote many interesting seashore books. It lives in a slimy tube buried in the sand, and lined with cast-off stinging capsules and sand. When disturbed, it quickly withdraws into the tube. This species has two sets of tentacles. Tube Anemones have been known to live up to forty years and are easy to keep in your aquarium.

Size: Body up to 20 cm; span of tentacles up to 7 cm
Where to look: Just below low water in mud or sand
Range: Most European waters; a different species in
Mediterranean

Cerianthus lloydi

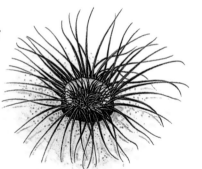

Johnstones' Ornate Worm

This worm lives in a thin, membranous tube to which sand and mud are stuck. Look out for long whitish threads stretching out from beneath a stone or over the mud in a pool. These are the worm's feeding tentacles and are all you will see unless you dig down to find the soft body. This type of worm is called a 'terebellid' and there are many similar species.

Size: Up to 25 cm
Where to look: Under muddy
rocks and in muddy sediments
Range: Most European coasts

Neoamphitrite figulus

Candy Stripe Flatworm

This is an attractive flatworm that, like its relatives, seems to flow over seaweeds or rock surfaces. If you look closely, you will see waves of movement ripple along its body as it moves forward. It has two sensory tentacles on its head end. Occasionally this worm may take off and swim for a short distance. It eats carrion and small animals.

Size: Up to 3 cm
Where to look: Under stones on muddy gravel;
often found on mussel beds
Range: Most European coasts

Prostheceraeus vittatus

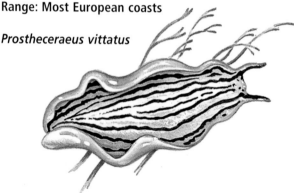

Peacock Worm

This worm is so-called because its disc of coloured tentacles are supposed to resemble a peacock's tail. It builds a tube from particles of mud and this is anchored at the bottom end to a stone. This tube sticks up some seven centimetres out of the mud, and the worm spreads its tentacles out of the top end to catch drifting food particles. If you disturb the water or let your shadow fall on it, the worm will instantly disappear back down into its tube.

Size: Mud tube up to 30 cm long; worm 8–15 cm
Where to look: On muddy and gravelly sand in sheltered places, especially in estuaries and shore shallows
Range: Most European coasts
Sabella **species**

Parchment Worm

This worm lives in a U-shaped tube under the sand, lined with the parchment-like material that gives it its common name. Both ends of the tube emerge about 4 cm above the surface. It has a series of paddles which propel water over its body to bring it food and oxygen. It makes a mucus 'net' which traps the food. Every few minutes, it rolls this into a ball and swallows it. This worm is luminous, but nobody has yet solved the mystery of why it is.

Size: Up to 25 cm long
Where to look: Rare on the tidal shore; often stranded after gales
Range: Most European coasts

Chaetopterus variopedatus

Striped Ribbon Worm

When relaxed, this is a very long worm, but, if disturbed, it will shrink to half its size. It is a species you will really have to look for because it burrows. The Striped Ribbon Worm has no bristles and its body is not divided by rings. It moves by a swelling that passes along its body. It eats carrion and small creatures.

Size: Up to 70 cm
Where to look: Lower shores; often partly buried in sand under a rock
Range: Most European coasts

Tubulanus annulatus

Bootlace worm

If you are looking forward to discovering a record, here is one to search for. This is the longest worm you will find on European coasts. You might find one coiled up in a tangle which is difficult to unravel. It catches prey, even fish, and holds on as its elastic body stretches and contracts until the prey tires. If you find one, measure its length.

Size: Up to several metres long
Where to look: Under stones on lower shores
Range: Northern European coasts

Lineus longissimus

Find Out Some More

Useful organizations

The best organization for you to get in touch with is your local County Wildlife Trust. There are over 40 of these trusts in Great Britain and you should contact them if you want to know about wildlife and nature reserves and activities in your area. Ask your local library for their address, or contact:

The Wildlife Trusts The Kiln, Waterside, Mather Road, Newark, Nottinghamshire NG24 1WT (0870 036 7711).

Wildlife Watch is the junior branch of The Wildlife Trusts. Local Wildlife Watch groups run meetings all over the country. Again you can find out about your nearest Wildlife Watch group by contacting The Wildlife Trusts.

Your local **natural history society** may organize visits to the seaside to find and study the animals. They are led by local experts and you will find them of great help. Your local library will have a list of them.

The Conchology Society of Great Britain & Ireland, 35 Bartlemy Road, Newbury, Berkshire RG14 6LD.

Marine Conservation Society, 9 Gloucester Road, Ross-on-Wye HR9 5BU (01989 566017). This charity campaigns for clean seas and beaches, and against the trade in rare shells and sea creatures. They work in conjunction with Wildlife Watch. They produce Fact Sheets on habitats, marine animals and pollution.

National Trust for Places of Historic Interest or Natural Beauty, 32 Queen Anne's Gate, London SW1H 9AB (01793 817400). For membership and enquiries: The National Trust, PO Box 39, Warrington WA5 7WD (0870 458 4000). They own more than 232,000 hectares of countryside throughout England, Wales and Northern Ireland. These include many woods, nature reserves and sites of special scientific interest. Most are open to visitors, but you usually have to pay to get in.

The National Trust also run courses with school groups; ask your teacher to find out about these. In Scotland, contact the Head of Education **The National Trust for Scotland**, Wemyss House, 28 Charlotte Square, Edinburgh EH2 4ET (0131 243 9300).

Places to visit

There are over 14,400 kilometres of coastline around Britain. Almost anywhere you go, you will find marine animals on the beach. In Europe, any beach along the Mediterranean should have many interesting species. The North Sea beaches of Holland and Germany are another good hunting ground. In Great Britain, try visiting:

Rocky pools and shores: The Seven Sisters, Sussex; Sheringham, Norfolk; Filey Brigg, N. Humberside; Boulmer Haven, Northumbria; Great Cumbrae Island, near Largs, Strathclyde; **Sand or mud flats:** Shell Bay, Studland Heath, Dorset; The Wash, Lincs; Red Rocks, West Kirby, Merseyside; Morcambe Bay, Lancs; **Estuaries and lagoons:** Chesil Beach, Dorset; River Orwell, near Ipswich, Suffolk; Cemlyn, near Amlwch, Gwynedd; River Humber, Humberside; Solway Firth, Dumfries & Galloway; Borth submerged forest, Dyfi National Nature Reserve, near Aberystwyth, Dyfed; **Intertidal rocks and sand:** Purbeck Marine Wildlife Reserve, Dorset; Oxwich, near Swansea, W. Glamorgan; Isle of Tyree, Strathclyde.

Index & Glossary

To find the name of an animal in this index, search under its main name. So, to look up Golden Cup Coral; look under 'Coral, Cup', not under 'Golden' or 'Cup'. Names of animal groups are shown like this: FISH.

Index & Glossary